SMALL IS YOUR SUPERPOWER!

How Small Businesses (Finally!) Can Outsmart Big Brands at Marketing

Shawna Suckow, CSP

Published by
PORCUS VOLANTI PRESS
A division of Flying Pig Innovations LLC

First Edition

ISBN (eBook):.979-8-9935226-0-9
ISBN (paperback): 979-8-9935226-1-6

Disclaimer

This book is for informational and educational purposes only. While I've done my best to make the advice helpful, practical, and based on real-world experience, it's not a substitute for professional legal, financial, or business advice tailored to your specific situation.

Every small business is different. Marketing strategies that work for one might flop for another. So before making big decisions based on what you read here, consider talking to a qualified professional who understands your business, your goals, and your market.

I'm not liable for any losses, gains, or superhero-level decisions you make based on this book. Use your powers wisely.

Praise for *Small is Your Superpower*

"Small is your Superpower *is so timely. Big brands are vulnerable to small companies who do smart marketing that plays to their strengths. Shawna explains why, gives you the strategy, and then provides examples. You can take this book and get right to work. If you run or are starting a small business, read it!"*

—Ian Lurie
Author of Web Marketing for Dummies©

"I started reading Small is your Superpower *and stopped after about 40 pages. I only stopped to grab my highlighter and begin re-reading this while taking notes! In a world crowded with management and self-help books, this is a how-to manual. Don't miss this one."*

—Jeffrey Chrzanowski
Product Strategist
HTC Inc.

"Small is Your Superpower *is dead on for what's going on in marketing."*

—Reid Holmes
Author of *Appreciated Branding*, Speaker, Consultant
House of Holmes Idea Labs

"Small is Your Superpower *has so much advice that we will use. I love it, because we need more humanity, reality, and basically more of 'us' and our personality in what we do. Thanks for the license to be us and show our superpowers."*

—Greg von der Ahe
EVP of Strategy & Key Accounts
Challenger Cable Sales

"Shawna empowers small business owners to see that their size—and their individuality—are their greatest strengths. She reminds us that being YOU is your superpower, and that authenticity, connection, and storytelling are what make a brand unforgettable. Shawna shares it all, showing you how to tell your story and stand out in a way big brands never can."

—Rachel Kane
Founder
WomenBusinessSpeakers.com

"After reading Shawna's book, I traced back the sources of marketing that I paid attention to. She's right, your time is now. I equate it to a running back expediting decisive cuts on the fly with "Presence, not polish."

—Christopher Coulthard
Business Manager
Rutgers University Press

Free Marketing Resources for My Readers

Reach out: hello@shawnasuckow.com

Hey there! You with the eyeballs!

Thanks for reading my book. As a gift to you to help implement the strategies, I've created a Superpower Vault with free resources you can access 24/7 (you know, during the wee hours of the night when you finally get a break from running the business). It's full of step-by-step marketing ideas, exercises, assessments, and done-for-you assets. You can access it anytime via this QR code or at www.bit.ly/superpowervault.

Want more marketing insights beyond the book?

Speaking (my favorite!)

If you want your audience to lean in, laugh while learning, and take real action after the event, that's my lane (plus, I'll keep them awake and engaged, so your coffee budget doesn't break the bank!). I bring outside perspective that shifts behavior, delivered with the candor of a true friend (the one who tells you when you have taco lettuce in your teeth). #NoBoringKeynotes

Business Book Clubs

I can pop into your discussion virtually, lead a session or entire series, or do an in-person launch or Q&A.

Marketing Superheroes Mastermind Group
A no-fluff, high-trust space where I lead small business owners in solving real marketing challenges and growing faster. Check out the vault to see when there's an opening to join.

Consulting (In Person or Remote)
If your marketing feels stale, confusing, or like you're shouting into the void (and it's not even echoing back...rude!), I'll step in as your outside brain and we'll get to the root of it and figure out what really works for your company (and you!).

One-on-One Coaching
For business owners or fellow speakers who want more traction and simplicity, my coaching is part marketing therapist, part strategy accelerator. We'll dig into what's working, what's not...and maybe what's been on that back burner for too long. You'll know exactly how to attract your **Exact Right Customers™**, and finally love your marketing.

One-Time 360° Marketing Assessment
Sometimes you just need a clear-eyed, no-fluff look at your entire marketing landscape. In my 360° Marketing Assessment, I audit everything—your website, social media, emails, swag, surveys, branding...bring it all on—to pinpoint what's helping you and what's quietly repelling customers. You'll get a detailed report delivered via Zoom so you can ask questions and really understand. Plus, my AI transcriber Bot (her name is Fatima), will send you a full recording with a list of recommendations and action steps. I'll give you the blueprint, you then go build it on your own schedule.

For Rob, Abbie, Maddie, Sophie, and Finn.
You make my life so much richer.

For every small business owner who quietly carries the weight, chases the dream, and keeps showing up for the people they serve.

Table of Contents

Foreword

We hear a lot about scale these days – how the biggest brands grab the headlines, flood the ad space, and shape the story. But here's the thing those headlines miss: smaller organizations are doing something the big guys can't. They're building trust. They're showing up in their communities. And they're creating real, meaningful connections.

In a previous role leading local marketing for a broadband operator with an 18-state footprint, I learned quickly that one-size-fits-all doesn't work. I visited 15 markets in just a few months to see what "local" really meant – and it changed everything. Each community had its own rhythm, its own voice, and its own superpower. That experience still shapes how I think about marketing today. Because when you understand what makes each place unique, you can show up in ways that truly matter.

Independent companies are proving every day that impact isn't about size. It's about heart, purpose, and the people behind the brand. These businesses may be lean, but they're powerful. And they're changing the game.

Small is Your Superpower celebrates that energy. Shawna Suckow doesn't offer fluff. She gives you a practical, inspiring guide to marketing with authenticity, creativity, and confidence. In a world full of noise, this book is a reminder that "real" still matters. And no one delivers "real" better than you.

As you flip through these pages, I hope you see your own story. I hope you feel encouraged to lean into what makes your organization different and know you're not alone. You're part of a movement that's redefining what marketing looks like.

Let's keep showing the world that small isn't a limitation – it's a superpower. And when we lead with purpose, we don't just compete...we connect!

Christy Drummond, VP Marketing
NCTC (National Content and Technology Cooperative)

PART I

The Rise of the Underdog

If you're holding this book, odds are you've already had it with traditional marketing. You're tired of spending hours creating social posts for multiple channels that get two likes (one from your mom). You've likely invested in flashy courses that promise all their million-dollar secrets. You've likely tried to emulate the Big Brands—with more people in their marketing department than you have in your entire business. You think they must have all the answers. And still? Nada.

> *It's not you. It's the whole marketing ecosystem, and the ecosystem has finally changed, in your favor.*

Big Brand marketing is outdated. Worse—it's disconnected. It was built for a different era, one when people trusted slogans, believed ads, and didn't have a built-in B.S.-detector defaulting to HIGH. But today's buyers have evolved. They scroll faster, trust slower, and have zero tolerance for salesyness. If your marketing still feels like a pitch, you've already lost them.

But finally, consumer evolution is working in your favor as a small business!

We are living through a rare business moment—call it the great marketing shift. Whether you're a solopreneur as I am, a micro-company of five people, or a small business with 50 employees, your marketing rules are being rewritten in real-time. Small businesses finally have a chance not just to compete, but to lead. Because when the old system starts to crumble, those small and nimble enough to move quickly and authentically will rise up. The crumble is well underway. This is your time.

Your Superpower? Being Small (and Real)

We're in a crisis of disconnection. A recent American Psychiatric Association poll found that 30% of U.S. adults feel lonely at least once a week[1]. Meanwhile, a Harvard study reported that 21% of Americans feel persistently disconnected—from friends, family, the world[2]. I personally feel like both those numbers are too low for what's really going on out there.

---

[1] American Psychiatric Association (2024). "APA Poll: One in Three Adults Report Frequent Loneliness." www.psychiatry.org/newsroom/news-releases/loneliness-in-americans-2024

[2] Harvard Loneliness Study (2024). "Disconnected: A National Study on Isolation and Its Mental Health Impacts." www.hsph.harvard.edu/news/press-releases/loneliness-survey-2024/

We're also in a trust crisis. I've been tracking how much consumers trust businesses for over 10 years, and it's at an all-time low now. In fact, I conducted a poll recently that shocked me. I asked, "Do you trust businesses more, less, or about the same as 10 years ago?"

98% said they trust businesses less!

That's why brands that sound less like businesses and more like messy, real, human people are thriving. We are starved for connection. We don't want a sleek sales funnel. We want proof of life behind the business. We want presence, not polish.

That's where you come in. You don't have to outspend your competitors. You just have to out-human them.

And right now, the businesses winning at marketing aren't louder—they're just willing to be real. People don't need another pitch. They need someone who actually sees them and speaks their language...and it isn't the language of perfection anymore.

Whether your business is B2B or B2C, this is the permission you've been waiting for: to stop generating "professional" content that sounds like everybody else, and start saying what your customers actually need to hear—in a voice and perspective that are unmistakably yours. Best of all, it's easy and cheap, because you already have everything you need.

That realness? It's your first true marketing advantage.

Superhero reference incoming (rest assured, there will be a few throughout these next chapters):
Your mild-mannered business has secretly become the superhero of trust-building. I say "secret" because most large brands haven't even caught on to this! And when they do finally catch on, they won't be able to replicate what you have.

Your Superhero Utility Belt Is Already Packed (Even If It Doesn't Feel Like It)

Big brands have layers of processes: marketing departments, external agencies, strict branding guidelines, and compliance departments. It's a miracle they manage to say anything at all. Meanwhile, you can wake up tomorrow, shoot a 60-second video about something you believe in, and post it. That's the real marketing edge today.

You have:

- **Speed:** You can generate material in minutes, not months.
- **Direct access:** You can actually talk to your customers—and listen.
- **Permission:** You don't have to follow corporate playbooks. You get to write your own.

You also have something even more important: instinct. You know when something sounds off. You know what your audience cares about because you talk to them—not through a focus group, but at the counter, on the phone, or via email, Zoom, chat, and social media. That connectedness is priceless.

And personality? You've got that. You can (and should!) let your weird show. That's what your customers are craving today—the real deal—and that's what will make you stand out, build trust, and become unforgettable.

You don't need a litany of brand guidelines. You need your personality, knowledge, and your cell phone camera (okay, maybe a couple energy drinks, too).

Is this book for B2B or B2C?

We as humans have evolved beyond traditional marketing—it just doesn't work on us anymore. It's the first time in the history of modern marketing that there's so little difference between the habits and desires of any type of buyer. Whether B2B or B2C, you won't see much difference, except in where you can find them. B2B hangs out on LinkedIn and at tradeshows; consumers hang out everywhere (including LinkedIn!).

Regardless of whether your customers are businesses or consumers, we're all trending in the same direction now: toward distrust, disconnection, and the desire for transparency and realness. The solutions in this book apply across the board, except where I've specifically noted otherwise. With that in mind, just for ease, I use 'customer' throughout the book to mean client, prospect, buyer, end-user.

Every Superhero Needs a Sidekick

Meet yours! Throughout this book, Sparky share quick tips and takeaways (Get it? Sparky – like a spark of an idea!).

THE SIDEKICK SAYS:

THINK OF ME LIKE YOUR OWN PERSONAL JARVIS, ALFRED, EDNA, OR AGENT 99 (BONUS POINTS IF YOU GET ALL FOUR REFERENCES). I'M HERE TO HELP YOU AMPLIFY WHAT'S ALREADY WORKING FOR YOU, AND GIVE YOU NEW TIPS FOR WHAT'S NOT.

SIDEBAR: What's the Deal with All the Dogs?

Dogs on the cover, the underdog theme, a dog for a sidekick…what's up with that? Well, when I finally gave myself permission years ago to stop trying to mirror the more established, successful speakers, I let my own style emerge. Part of that is including dogs in all my slides when delivering a keynote. I also mercilessly tease cats (and cat people…sorry, not sorry!). When I explain this to my audiences, I give two simple reasons:

1. Because dogs.
2. Because not cats.

Bringing my unique personality and style to my work has made all the difference in my success as a speaker, consultant, coach, and small business owner. It's also what I'm asking you to do in your small business. I'm simply walking the talk. I'm not for everyone, and neither should you be. As they say, there are riches in the niches.

What if You're Not a Content Creator?

Customers aren't loyal to big corporate institutions anymore—they're loyal to people. Or more accurately, to businesses that show up like people.

> *And before you start thinking, "That sounds nice, but I'm not a content creator,"* **stop right there** *(anyone else reminded of 'Paradise by the Dashboard Lights' when you read that?). You don't need to be a professional Content Creator. You just need to be human on purpose. To create posts that sound like something you'd say. To film a selfie video that sounds like a conversation, not a commercial. To answer a DM like you're texting a friend, not pitching a service.*

The businesses that do this today don't just stand out. They stick. They last. They grow through word of mouth, customer loyalty, and repeat business. Because they're not built on tactics. They're built on truth.

This is Really Important

You're going to hear me say this a lot: being small is no longer a disadvantage. But in this new marketing era, you need more than just size on your side. You need a new strategy built around:

- Standing out in a world of noise
- Building real trust with the most skeptical customers ever
- Creating marketing that people actually remember

That's what this book will cover. You'll learn why small businesses are suddenly in the best position to connect, convert, and outmaneuver the giants. You'll see how the big guys are getting it all wrong—and why their biggest weakness is your biggest opportunity. And then, we'll dive into the concept I call **Customer Brandships™**—my framework that simplifies what great marketing looks like now.

If you've ever felt like you were doing everything "right" and still getting ignored, this book is your reset button. A way to finally make sense of what matters now.

It's time to stop playing by someone else's rules—and start building a marketing game plan that's true to you.

Because small isn't your challenge anymore...

...it's your *superpower.*

Summary

- Traditional marketing playbooks are failing because they ignore how people really think, feel, and buy today.
- The new advantage belongs to small businesses who act like humans, not huge corporations.
- You don't need a bigger ad budget. You need a clearer, humanized voice.
- Trust, connection, and unforgettable presence are your new marketing superpowers.

Action Steps

1. Write down three things your business does that are 100% human (even if they seem too small to matter).
2. Look at your last email or social post. Would your best friend say it sounds like you?
3. Make a list of your current marketing materials. You'll need them to reference as we move along.

Remember, anytime you need help, visit the Superpower Vault for free resources: www.bit.ly/superpowervault

CHAPTER 1

Small is Your Superpower

"Small" used to feel like an insult in the business world. It was like being told you had a "nice personality." The narrative for decades was 'bigger is better.' Bigger teams, bigger budgets, bigger buildings. Everything in the business world used to revolve around scale.

If you said you worked alone, or had a team of five, or even 20, you were met with the kind of nod my kids reserve for me when I try to use GenZ slang (as in, "Aww, isn't it cute but pathetic how she's trying?").

But then something interesting happened...the rules changed, and almost no one noticed. Customers changed, the trust crisis grew, and the slick, polished, uber-professional campaigns that once ruled the marketing landscape started to fall flat. We stopped needing brands to inspire us with sleek perfection and started craving brands that could just be real with us.

While big brands were (and still are) putting out perfect ads full of perfect people doing things perfectly, a few brave small businesses started getting real. They stopped trying to sound bigger and started showing up as themselves. They got closer to their customers. They came across more human. And we the Consumers? We loved it. We started choosing heart over hype.

Think of the influencers who currently fill your social media feed. They're likely real people who show up just chatting with you like you're a friend in the same room. They show up messy and imperfect. Sure, there will always be Kim Kardashians, but there are thousands of real, imperfect human beings out there building huge followings and selling a lot of merch by just being relatable and trustworthy.

What used to be your biggest frustration and limitation—your size—is now your greatest marketing strength. You are officially cleared for takeoff (I'm thinking of Wonder Woman's invisible airplane here, and I have so many questions...but I digress).

The Trust Gap: Why Big Is Breaking Down

We're not just in a marketing trend shift—we're in a trust crisis. According to the recent Edelman Trust Barometer, trust in major brands has dropped by a staggering 31% since 2020 (and it was already nosediving before then).

People aren't just skeptical—their B.S. detectors are constantly on high alert now. It's not enough to say you're the best anymore. You have to show up in ways that feel believable, relatable, and true.

Remember the scene from Elf where Buddy sees the sign in the café window that says something like, 'World's Best Coffee'? He runs in to congratulate them and everybody just stares at him. That's how consumers feel today when any company claims that they're the best, without legitimate proof.

Cue the Dawn of the Small Business Era...

That same Edelman report shared that 74% of people now say they're more likely to buy from a small business even if it costs more. That's huge news! Why? Because they believe small businesses are more honest, more responsive, and more invested in the people they serve, and they're not wrong.

Consumers today are navigating what can only be described as sheer marketing overload. They're hit with 10,000 marketing messages every day[3]—emails, ads, notifications, influencer content, blog posts, pop-ups, and creepy website tracking. It's only gotten worse with the advent of A.I. because it's made everything so easy to generate in volume. The result? So much of the marketing content out there just feels...empty.

When consumers feel the weight of all this overload, every day, their first instinct isn't to engage. It's to run. To block, delete, or

[3] Source: Salesforce, "2024 State of the Connected Customer" www.salesforce.com

scroll on by. Because everyone's shouting, but very few are saying anything that feels remotely real.

Big companies try to solve this problem by throwing money at it. They hire consultants to tell them how to "humanize the brand." They obsess over their social media stats while never speaking to an actual customer unless it's during a focus group.

They think sincerity can be conveyed by the right lighting, brand colors, and fonts. They study our psychology and tweak accordingly.

People, though, can sniff out scripted emotions today. You can't fake real. Not anymore. Not when the public has seen behind the curtain and knows exactly how the sausage is made (eww).

Some of the most tone-deaf marketing in the past few years came from the biggest brands. Remember all the companies that posted "We're all in this together" during the pandemic while simultaneously announcing mass layoffs and getting government bailouts? That's what I mean when I say there's a trust crisis. And the crisis is getting deeper.

But here's the interesting part: you're standing on the side of the trust gap where people still believe. They still believe in local, handmade, and human-focused. They believe in "I'll call you back today" instead of "your request is important to us."

This is where you come in. Because as a small business, you *are* people. You're not hiding behind layers of departments and approvals. You're in the thick of it. You're answering emails, shaking hands, remembering customer names and that they mentioned their daughter's graduation next month. That's not a CRM reminder—that's connection.

Your size lets you build trust faster and deeper than any multi-million-dollar ad campaign. Your conversations are your content. Your reputation is your marketing strategy. And your stories are the foundation of it all.

So while the big guys keep brainstorming ways to manufacture sincerity, you just need to keep showing up as yourself. Because in this era, trust isn't something you buy, it's something you earn. And you've already got the inside track.

What Size Really Gets You

Being small in business used to mean being left out. Left out of industry panels, media articles, and trade show keynote slots that went to the guy with nothing relevant to say, because he hasn't spoken to actual customers in years.

> *Today, small is finally being seen for what it truly is: nimble, smart, and scrappy.*

What you lack in budget you make up for in speed. What you lack in headcount you make up for in heart. You've probably made business decisions in the middle of dinner, on a walk, or from the front seat of your car while trying not to spill a coffee. That's agility.

Being small lets you skip the corporate mask and just show up. You can break the fourth wall. You can—and should—be honest when things don't go as planned, and people will lean in closer, not walk away. Because honesty in a world of marketing-spin is magnetic.

Big brands spend millions of dollars trying to replicate what you can do with one well-written email and a funny video. And that's not an exaggeration. That's the reality of the new business landscape.

So instead of seeing your size as something to overcome, start seeing it as your advantage. *Your customers already do.*

This Moment Was Made for You

Every so often, the world gets one of those rare inflection points—times when the old way falls apart just enough to let something better emerge. This is one of those times.

What used to be your uphill battle—getting noticed, getting traction, getting taken seriously—is about to get a lot easier. Because attention spans have shortened, skepticism has risen, and audiences are craving what big brands can't deliver: nuance, imperfection, and human-to-human interaction. Welcome to your moment.

Here's why this era is tailor-made for small businesses:

1. **The democratization of tools.** Five years ago, you needed a creative agency or special equipment to shoot a decent

video. The pandemic changed all that. Our world became more casual (cue the cats rudely walking across your keyboard on a Zoom call...). Now, you just need the nerve to hit record. A.I. tools let you brainstorm content. Canva lets you design like a pro. Scheduling tools let you build systems that once required full teams. You've got more tools at your disposal than most CMOs had in their entire career fifteen years ago, and you can use them faster.

2. **Culture is exhausted.** People are tired of being marketed to. They're tired of the pitch and the polish. What they want is to *feel* something when they interact with a brand. That's hard for the big guys, but second nature for small businesses. You're used to talking about real problems and celebrating real wins. You're already halfway there.

3. **The bar is surprisingly low.** I mean this kindly (well, not really): your competition is boring or confusing or too professional. If you can be slightly more interesting than a laundry basket, you're ahead. If you can be clear, helpful, and a little funny, you're unforgettable.

4. **Relationship over reach.** Once upon a time, marketing was about blasting the message to the masses. Now it's about creating meaningful touchpoints with the right people. You likely don't need 100,000 followers. You need 10,000 or 1,000 or even just 100 (depending on your business model) loyal humans who get you, trust you, and refer you. Big

brands can't pivot to this model without blowing up their entire structure. You're already built for it.

5. **People want a story they can believe in.** The story where the person behind the product shows up, tells the truth, and keeps showing up—even when it's hard. You have hundreds of interesting stories (don't roll your eyes, you really do). It's time to tell them, and I'll help.

This moment belongs to the small and scrappy (note to self: stop using that word. It reminds me of Scrappy Doo - worst sidekick ever added to a cartoon).

This moment belongs to the brands with personality, perspective, and the guts to say, "This is who we are, and we're not trying to be anything else." This is your advantage.

And if you've ever caught yourself thinking, "I don't have a team like they do,"—let me stop you right there.

THE SIDEKICK SAYS:

YOU DON'T NEED TO BE MORE LIKE THEM. THEY NEED TO BE MORE LIKE YOU.

Let's dive into it, shall we?

CHAPTER 2

What Big Companies Don't Get (and Why They Can't Do What You Can)

If you've ever found yourself scrolling through a big brand's social media feed and thought, "Did a robot write this?"—you're not alone. Across platforms and industries, customers are quietly backing away from the over-produced, the over-polished, and the overly rehearsed. They're not just craving real, they're demanding it.

You've probably felt this in your gut for a while now. Maybe it was when you saw a local company's sandwich board saying something funny. Or maybe it was when you saw a small business owner reply to an online customer complaint with such grace and honesty that you thought, "Now that's how it's done."

I can't overemphasize what a seismic shift this is. According to a recent Global Trust Pulse Report, 7 out of 10 consumers say they've *stopped buying* from brands that "feel disconnected from real people." Let that sink in. Customers are literally ghosting billion-dollar companies in favor of businesses that remember their name and speak like humans.

We're in a new marketing era now—one where emotional content beats ad spend, and being human beats being huge. This chapter is here to help you understand exactly why big brands are failing at connection and why they literally *can't* replicate what you do so naturally.

I need you to know that you're not behind any eight-ball. You're not playing catch-up anymore. You're finally ahead of the curve. And every awkward, unfiltered, beautifully real thing about how you show up online? That's your new edge.

Let's dig into what's really going on behind the curtain of the big guys—and why this is your moment to take the cape and fly.

The Performance Problem

Most big brand marketing today is a performance. A well-rehearsed, highly funded, legally approved performance designed to check boxes and appeal to everyone while offending no one. It's perfect, and perfectly safe.

These companies are running their marketing like a Broadway show: scripted lines, perfect actors, and faked emotions. But today's audience isn't looking for a show; they're looking for a conversation. They don't want to watch a brand perform. They want to interact with a business that feels present, responsive, and relatable.

Take the customer service department of any large company. Their favorite word? “Unfortunately.”

“Unfortunately, that’s outside our policy.”
“Unfortunately, we can’t help you at this time.”
“Unfortunately, your call is important to us but not important enough to answer.”

Compare that to a local bakery owner replying to a 2-star review with, “Yikes. That doesn’t sound like us—thank you for pointing it out. Can we send you a better cookie and try again?” One reply builds resentment. The other builds brand equity. Guess which one the customer screenshots and shares? Both, for very different reasons.

Big brands have nailed down how to be everything to everyone, but when they do that, they’re nothing special to anyone.

According to a 2025 global study by Attentive, “81% of consumers ignore irrelevant marketing messages, and aren’t just indifferent to generic marketing—they actively disengage if messages aren't relevant.”[4] That’s not just disengagement, it’s

---

[4] Attentive.com (2025) “New Global Study Reveals Consumers Demand More Personalization in Marketing” www.attentive.com

disdain. And that's a gap you can breakdance right into (sorry, not sorry...GenX here) with your honest, unfiltered energy.

You, the small business owner with a phone camera—you're not performing. You're reacting to comments in real-time. You're posting without a committee. You're emailing your list like you'd email a friend. That's what audiences crave now: not the showiness.

When you do it, it's effortless, engaging, and trusted.

So while big brands choreograph every syllable, you get to improvise. You get to show up as yourself. And that, my friend, is the real stuff your prospects crave.

The Trust Gap

Let's talk about the one thing your future customers *aren't* saying out loud:

"I really want to trust you... but I've been burned before."

Just like our foster dog, Larry. He came to us after being rescued from the mean streets of Minneapolis. He was bounced from the pound to two more places before landing with us. He so wanted to trust us, but he'd been through a lot. (Happy ending – after a month with us, he found his furever family!).

But that's what we're up against. We live in an era where people have a long memory for bad businesses. Trust today isn't optional if you want repeat business, or even first-time customers. It's *non-negotiable.*

In fact, 81% of consumers say they need to trust a brand before even considering a purchase[5]. The larger or more personal the purchase, the truer that becomes.

What the Data Actually Shows

- **The Trust Deficit**
  A recent PwC Trust Survey found a massive gap: 84% of executives believe their company is highly trusted, yet only 30% of consumers agree[6]. That's a 54-point blind spot!

- **Small Business Trust Advantage**
  According to an Exploding Topics report, 86% of consumers say authenticity is vital[7]. You're already set up to meet that need as a small business. Most small businesses just need to give themselves permission to be authentic. We'll get there.

---

[5] Exploding Topics, "33 Branding Statistics and Trends for 2025," *81% need trust before buying* (explodingtopics.com)

[6] PwC, "2024 Trust Survey: Execs vs Consumers"

[7] Exploding Topics, Top Branding Statistics for 2025: *86% say authenticity matters* (influencermarketinghub.com)

- **Digital Trust Is Fragile**
  PwC also found that 40% of consumers stopped buying from a brand due to mistrust[8]. But if they already trust you when you mess up, and then you fix it, they're more likely to be forgiving because of that trust.

How the Trust Gap Hurts You

Your audience hears the noise. They've been ghosted by big companies, burned by shady business practices, and turned off by big brand scandals and misdeeds. So when they see any form of glossy advertising, their internal voice whispers, *"Here we go again."*

That means every business starts in the *red* trust-wise. You're not just competing for attention; you're competing for fragile trust.

A Fictional Case Study: Toothy Grin Dental – Lakewood, Colorado

Toothy Grin Dental—run by Dr. Bonni and her team in Lakewood, CO (shout out to my hometown!)—decided to turn trust into a strategy:

---

[8] PwC, *40% stop buying* (thegreatentrepreneurs.com)

- They started promising to answer appointment requests via a new website chat option within 30 minutes (often instantly, but, you know, those pesky patients in the office keep wanting attention!).
- They implemented the ability for patients to communicate via text, and their patients love it (especially Gen Y and Gen Z).
- They launched a monthly newsletter that included real patient journeys—not just perfect ones. A Pet of the Month photo. A non-dental related 'Mom Tip' from the office manager, because she's a mom of five, and this dental practice knows many of their patients are families.

Why Big Brands Can't Compete Here

Big companies can test market trust with $100K surveys—but they don't *live* it. That means while you may not have their Fortune 500 budget, your honesty and clarity can close the trust gap faster—even more effectively.

How to Close the Gap—Actively

- **Be super responsive**: Set a response window and honor it—even if it's a quick "Got your message, we're on it!" auto-reply.

- **Mess Up/Fess up**: If you make a mistake, admit it quickly. "Oops—we had an inventory issue and disappointed you. Here's how we're fixing it."
- **Share your journey**: Behind-the-scenes updates go far: "Here's a peek at our sleek new in-office gizmo! You may not think it's cool, but we're nerding out over here."
- **Show real voices**: Skip jargon. Use first-person: "I," "me," "we"—not "ABC Company."

Little gestures add up. Each is another deposit in your customers' bank of trust.

Why It Matters

If they believe you *care*, they'll remember, return, and recommend.

The Trust Gap isn't just a challenge—it's your **opportunity**. Lean into trust. Do what big brands can't: be *present*, *transparent*, and *personable*—every single day, with every single message.

You Can't Fake Empathy

If there's one thing big brands love more than a meeting that could have been an email, it's talking about how "customer-centric" they are. They'll plaster it on in-store posters, insert it into every press release, and even build entire ad campaigns around the phrase "we care." But caring isn't a slogan; it's a skill. And frankly, it's one most of them will never master.

> *One exception: The big pet care brand, Chewy. Did you know they send flowers to every customer when a pet dies? They include a handwritten note of sympathy. There must be other big companies that are good at empathy, but none come to mind - that's how rare it is!*

Real empathy isn't a PR stunt. It's what kicks in when a customer sends you a panicked email on a Saturday, and instead of forwarding it to a support team in another time zone, you answer it yourself—maybe with your kid on your hip and your dinner going cold. You do it not because it's strategic, but because it's *right*.

That kind of responsiveness is rare, and in a world flooded with fake apologies and delayed "thank you for your feedback" responses, it's unforgettable.

> *Here's what the data says: In a recent survey, "73% of consumers avoid businesses that don't show empathy."*[9]

Consumers today can instantly tell when a brand's empathy is scripted or performative, and they're over the polished pity.

---

[9] Zurich Insurance (2025) Study reveals empathy is the competitive edge companies shouldn't ignore" www.zurichinsurance.com

And presence isn't all that scalable—at least not the way big companies try to do it. You can't put "care" into a spreadsheet. Empathy happens in the in-between moments, the off-script responses, and a hand-written card when a customer least expects it.

You don't need a customer service script to sound human. You *are* human.

That's what makes your business feel not like an enterprise, but more like a group of people out to solve your customers' challenges.

Let's walk through a real-world contrast.

A customer emails a massive brand because their item was damaged in shipping. They get a robotic response: "We're sorry you're disappointed. Please visit our returns portal." Not exactly warm and fuzzy.

Now imagine that same complaint hits your inbox. You reply personally: "Oh no, that's definitely not okay—and not how we roll. I'm sending a new one out today and tossing in a little something extra for the hassle." The difference? One leaves the customer annoyed. The other leaves them loyal. Both scenarios might lead them to share their experience on social media, but yours wins hands down.

Big brands can't match that because their systems *aren't built* for it. Their metrics reward speed and volume, not connection.

Your advantage? You can slow down and take that extra couple minutes to write a sentence that doesn't sound like it came from a template.

Here's a bonus stat: "62% of consumers expect brands to deliver personalized content, while 67% feel frustrated when interactions lack relevance."[10] You don't need a viral moment. You need *meaningful ones*—on purpose, over time.

So the next time you wonder if empathy matters in your marketing, remember: It's not an extra. It's an edge. It's the thing people remember *after* the sale. And it's the thing most big brands never can deliver authentically—no matter how many consultants they hire.

They Can't Adapt Quickly (But You Can!)

Here's the scene: A trending song blows up on TikTok. Within hours, influencers all over the world are using it to show behind-the-scenes clips, poke fun at industry quirks, or promote their offers. Meanwhile, the marketing director of MegaCorp Inc. is still waiting for the social media compliance committee to approve a TikTok idea from three weeks ago.

This is your speed advantage. Big companies? Not so much.

---

[10] Sobot (2025) "Personalized Approaches Driving Customer Retention Success" www.sobot.com

Big means slow. Big means siloed. Big means a never-ending game of voicemail tag between departments to get approval on that idea for a holiday promotion six months from now.

But you see a comment, you tweak the offer. You notice an email isn't converting, you rewrite it. You hear a customer's pain point in a DM, and you immediately brainstorm a solution. That kind of responsiveness? Big brands *envy* it. But they can't replicate it. They're too tangled in their own structure.

Here's what that actually can look like.

You run a small email test campaign and see that the open rate sucks. You rewrite it. The click-throughs improve. You shifted in real time based on the feedback from just 20 people. And suddenly, your micro-list outperforms their mega-list. Not because you're better funded, because you're *better informed*—by your audience, in real time, while they're still holding focus groups.

> SIDEBAR: My take on Big Data these days is that it's instantly outdated when the report hits their desk. It's a look back at a moment in time when our world and our marketplace is shifting more rapidly than ever. That's not to say data is irrelevant; my point is that you have an actual handle on your customers and don't need expensive reports to prove what you already know.

Customers don't expect perfection anymore. They expect responsiveness. They want to feel seen. Heard. Considered. And when you change course quickly based on their needs, you're not just adjusting—you're *earning trust*.

Another superhero reference! Think of yourself like Ant-Man—small, agile, adaptable, and able to respond in a way The Hulk never could. You don't need size. You need small, smart moves, and you've got them.

The world doesn't reward the biggest voices anymore—it rewards the ones who listen and adapt. I like to think of it as the democratization of marketing—finally!

Humanity > Hashtags

You can spot a big brand's post from a mile away. It's perfectly filtered, carefully worded, and safe. Packed with jargon and hashtags. The caption: "Empowering inclusive solutions for future-forward alignment. #inclusive #solutions #alignment" The vibe: huge eye roll and a heavy sigh.

Now contrast that with a local business owner who posts, "This is my face after pulling a 14-hour day and realizing I still have 3 orders to pack. Running on caffeine, chaos, and possibly regret for staying up too late last night binge-watching Netflix." That's the post that gets shared. That's the post that gets saved. That's the post that gets customers rooting for you.

> *According to a recent report from Planoly, "In an age dominated by faceless corporations, behind-the-scenes content humanizes brands and organizations. By showcasing the people behind the products and services, companies foster transparency and trust with their customers."*[11]

This is where small business marketing truly shines—not in the perfect, but in the personal.

You're not just showing products, you're showing the process. You're not just showing wins, you're showing the work that goes into them. That matters. Because when people see the sweat behind the scenes, they believe in you more. They trust you more. And they *remember* you more.

You might not have a content team, or a lighting crew, or contracts with influencers. But you have what no algorithm can replicate: real, living, breathing presence.

Anyone can buy visibility, but they can't buy relatability.

Yet another superhero reference! Think of yourself like Peter Parker—stumbling through the day but always getting back up and doing the right thing. It's his *relatability*. He's just a kid trying to do his best, and we root for him because we've all been there.

---

[11] Planoly (2024) "Why Behind-The-Scenes Content is So Engaging" www.planoly.com

So while the big brands keep aiming for virality, you get to keep showing up with a little mess, a little heart, and a whole lot of human. And trust me—human wins every time.

Summary

Big brands may have the budgets, the teams, and the PR machines—but they don't have the most important currency in marketing today: trust, adaptability, and humanity. You've got those in spades.

While they're perfecting their "brand voice," you're using your *actual* voice. While they're running a five-week approval process, you're running laps around them with content that connects. While they're performing empathy, you're practicing it.

This is just another of your many superpowers.

Welcome to the new era of marketing. It's like it was made for you...because it is!

Action Steps

1. **Audit a Recent Post**
   Look at your last few blogs or social posts. Do they sound like a performance, or a person?

2. **Share the Human Stuff**
   Pick one "human moment" this week—whether it's a mistake or a messy behind-the-scenes snapshot—and share it with your audience.

3. **Be Loud About Your Smallness**
   Post something that only a small business *could* say. Use it to connect, not convert. Think: vulnerable, funny, relatable.

4. **Build Trust in the Comments**
   Respond to customer comments like a person, not a bot. Every interaction is a tiny brick in the foundation of long-term trust.

THE SIDEKICK SAYS:

PEOPLE FORGET PROMOTIONS. THEY REMEMBER EMOTIONS.

CHAPTER 3

The Top Three Marketing Challenges

Let's start with the three overarching marketing challenges that every business faces:

1. **Being Different Enough to Stand Out Amidst All the Noise**
2. **Building Real Trust**
3. **Being Unforgettable Enough to Matter**

We'll unpack each of these—like peeling the layers of an onion, except this onion is fun, friendly, and doesn't make you cry (unless you're weeping happy tears because you just love branding so much). Later in the book, I'll show you how successfully achieving these three goals builds toward something really valuable: Customer Brandships™.

Challenge One – Differentiation

You know that feeling when you open your inbox and it looks like Black Friday—chaotic, yelling, jostling for attention? That's your customers' daily reality with all the marketing noise. And that's what you're up against.

As I mentioned earlier, the average person these days sees around **10,000 marketing messages a day**. And we're not just talking about subtle messages. We're talking pop-ups, push notifications, banner ads, retargeting emails, sponsored reels, SMS blasts, and more, all in their face, all the time.

And in that avalanche of attention-grabbing nonsense, your little business has to elbow its way in and whisper, "Hey...notice me!"

Impossible? Not even a little.

Truth bomb: Big brands don't stand out anymore because they *can't afford to be weird*. They have shareholders and boardrooms. They must be all things to all people and never turn any customer off.

You, on the other hand, have the amazing freedom of targeting only what I call your **Exact Right Customers** (more on that later).

You have *personality*. You can—and should—take the chances the big guys can't. You can make people smile, think, or even spit out their coffee laughing.

That's standing out.

Example: let's compare two dental practices.

Here's a real quote from Google (practice's name changed to protect their...um...marketing mediocrity):

"[Redacted] Dental is a comprehensive solution for all your dental needs, including general and cosmetic dentistry, implants, dentures, and orthodontics."

Meanwhile, over on TikTok and Instagram, the dentists and staff of Aesthetic Family Dental Care in Arizona put out funny videos of dentists actually being...funny (check out one of my favorites posted on 8-13-25). They have 247,000 followers on TikTok and 73,000 on Instagram as of this printing. Do you think [Redacted] Dental comes anywhere close?

Interestingly, one of Aesthetic's videos dated 8-5-25 has this in the captions: "A lot of the dental industry thinks we are an embarrassment and should only be posting things about dental work. No Twerking and dancing like teenagers. Haters."

My point exactly! The majority of the industry is posting sameness and playing it safe, while these guys are differentiating themselves. Is it risky? Yes, in some ways:

1. Obviously, this strategy risked their professional reputation among colleagues, so they had to accept that going in.

2. Some of their videos are edgy with dance moves and colorful language, so they knew they would alienate some more...um...conventional patients.
3. They definitely shattered traditional marketing boundaries amongst medical practices, and there's no going back.

But 274,000 followers. Millions of views.

Best of all, letting their personalities out to play clearly has brought some fun to the office and their staff, and they're undoubtedly attracted more of their **Exact Right Customers** and repelled the kind they really don't want. Their videos likely put nervous patients at ease before they even enter the building—another bonus.

As I'll continue to say, it's not about going viral (but it certainly doesn't hurt!). Now, granted, the majority of those followers aren't in their geographic area, but I bet many have forwarded videos to people they know.

See the difference? One's blatantly bland. The other's relatable.

When you lean into your voice—your actual voice, you give people a reason to listen. You earn their attention by *deserving it*, not demanding it.

Exact Right Customers, You Say?

Your Exact Right Customers are the ones who just get you. They're loyal, enthusiastic, and eager to tell others about you—not because you begged for referrals, but because you made their lives easier, better, or more fun. These are the people who light you up and make all the long hours worthwhile.

Trying to be "for everyone" is the fastest way to lose the magic that makes you unforgettable. The second you water down your message to please the masses, you start sounding like the Big Brands—generic, predictable, and painfully forgettable. You can't afford to play in their sandbox, and honestly, you're too interesting to try. So get laser-focused on the people who love your flavor of awesome—and build your marketing to attract more like them.

Here's my spicy take: it's not just okay to repel the wrong customers—it's necessary. The wrong ones drain your energy, nitpick every detail, haggle over price, and make you question why you started this business in the first place. When you stop chasing them, you make room for the ones who actually value what you bring to the table. So don't worry if your marketing doesn't please everyone. It's filtering out the bad and attracting more of the good.

Leveraging Storytelling

The *less* you sound like a big brand, the *more* people trust you. According to a 2024 TrustPulse study, brands that use "first-person storytelling" in their content had 57% higher engagement rates than those that used traditional third-person "brand voice" narration.

Think about that. Your quirky caption about why you're tired but still packing orders? That's 57% more powerful than a million-dollar campaign.

So yes, there's noise. But you've got humanity, and that's having a million-dollar megaphone.

> *Superhero reference:* Think of my personal favorite, Deadpool. He's not trying to blend in. He's breaking the fourth wall, cracking jokes, and being completely himself. That makes him, in my opinion, the most unforgettable Marvel character to enter the movie theater in decades.

Challenge Two — Building Real Trust, Not Just Vibes

Marketing today has a trust problem. And no, it's not because people are cynical (though they are) or because everyone's burned out (they are, too). It's because most of us have been pitched to death.

Seriously. We've been promised younger skin, better abs, effortless success, and a six-figure lifestyle just by clicking "Buy Now." And to make it worse, nobody gives out free Ginsu knives with an order anymore (everyone over 50 knows what I'm talking about).

But then—every once in a while—a brand shows up that feels different. It doesn't yell. It doesn't spam. It doesn't seem like it's trying too hard. It just connects.

You lean in. You think, "Wow, they actually get me." And just like that, without a funnel or a nurture sequence or a lead magnet in sight, trust starts to form.

This is what happens when a customer feels understood before they've been *sold at*. It's that spark of alignment that turns a prospect into a buyer—not because you pushed hard, but because you showed up *real*.

Let's pause and be clear: this isn't fluffy marketing magic. It's not some ethereal "brand essence" thing. This is the core function of marketing that *works*. According to the same recent Edelman Trust Barometer report I cited in the last chapter, 74% of consumers say they're more likely to buy from a brand they believe "truly understands their needs and values." That's a business strategy that's truly easy for you, because you know your customers.

THE SIDEKICK SAYS:

TRUST ISN'T BUILT THROUGH FLAWLESS PHOTOS OR PERFECT MESSAGING. IT'S BUILT THROUGH REAL, IMPERFECT, HUMAN COMMUNICATION.

People today don't want to be pitched at, they want to be understood.

Think about your own habits. You ignore most ads, right? But when a brand shows up speaking your language, sharing your pet peeves, maybe even telling a story so close to your own, it's a little uncanny? You don't scroll past, you lean in. You subscribe and you instinctively trust them.

That's more than marketing. That's a relationship. In fact, it's a Customer Brandship™ (more on that to come).

Big brands struggle with this because they're addicted to polish. But all that perfection doesn't build trust, it erodes it.

But you can be real. You can send the email that gets people nodding. You can reply to a DM like a human, not a bot. You can show up in your sweatshirt on a Zoom call and still be the most trusted person in the (virtual) room.

Trust is built in the small moments.

The quick reply. The unexpected thank-you. The behind-the-scenes photo. The honest "we're figuring this out" update. Those are the moments that make customers feel like insiders, not outsiders.

And here's the business case: Trusted relationships hold up under pressure. They survive the hiccups. They can withstand economic dips, supplier delays, team changes, even price increases. Because when people *trust* you, they'll stick with you.

They're not just there for the deal. They're there for *you.*

Want a practical example?

Let's say you're a coach who sent out an email blast that unfortunately arrived to every prospect as "Dear [NAME]". Instead of pretending it didn't happen, you send a follow-up: "Well, that didn't go how I thought it would. And hey—if you're still reading this, thanks for sticking around, [NAME]. Just kidding." That honesty is small business gold. That's what keeps people engaged, even when the campaign goofed (ask me how I know).

Or you're a product business and your restock is delayed. You send an email that says, "Our supplier ghosted us and we're embarrassed. We're catching up, and gratefully thank you for your patience!" That kind of tone keeps your community with you—even when things don't go according to plan.

This type of marketing doesn't require perfection. It just requires *presence.*

If your campaigns aren't converting, or your content feels like it's disappearing into the void, the answer isn't more noise. It's more meaning.

Challenge Three – Being Unforgettable

Let's play a game. Try to remember one ad you saw yesterday.

Go ahead, I'll wait.

Tough, isn't it?

Despite being bombarded by 10,000 marketing messages per day, most people can't recall a single one unless it was hilariously bad or suspiciously weird (looking at you, AI-generated photo with twelve fingers). And therein lies the final frontier of small business marketing: being unforgettable enough to matter.

The real danger today isn't that your marketing fails. It's that they forget it instantly (like my high school locker combination in a strange recurring dream I've had for decades).

So how do you make your message stick?

It starts with understanding this truth: being liked is not the same as being remembered.

Big and small brands have a way of playing it so safe they become invisible. The result? Nothing offensive. Nothing too weird. Nothing real.

You, however, have the advantage of unpredictability if you're willing to step outside your comfort zone just a little. You're not bound by a reputation department. You get to say something *interesting*. You get to be *human*. You get to stand out by being—you know—*yourself*.

Being unforgettable doesn't come from polish. It comes from personality.

Ever get a thank-you note from a small business that actually made you think, 'wow – companies still do this?' Or see a photo on social media of the people at your favorite local coffee shop who just won a 'Best Of' award, and you feel proud of them (not like the Elf analogy)? That's the stuff people remember.

And that's where your real marketing muscle lives: in the moments you made someone *feel* something. Emotion equals retention.

Want to be remembered? Start with one of these:

- Make them laugh. (Like a snarky product description or an outtake from a failed product shoot.)
- Make them nod. (Share something honest and specific that makes them say, "Ugh, same.")
- Make them curious. (Lead with a question nobody else is brave enough to ask.)
- Make them feel seen. (Reflect a problem or habit so clearly, they wonder if you have hidden cameras.)

According to Stanford Marketing Professor Jennifer Aaker, **content with emotional storytelling is 22x more likely to be remembered than fact-based or product-focused messaging**[12].

---

[5] "Harnessing the Power of Stories" (www.womensleadership.stanford.edu)

And no, that's not a typo. Twenty-two times more unforgettable just by telling a good, real, human story.

In other words, "just the facts" marketing isn't just boring—it's forgettable. And forgettable is fatal today.

Big brands spend millions trying to simulate what you can do for free: connect with people in a way that feels real and sticks around.

That quirky reel you posted with your kid interrupting you mid-pitch? That's more unforgettable than a Super Bowl ad to the right audience.

That off-the-cuff social post where you shared a hard day, a win, or a weird customer interaction? That's the one that gets replies like, "I've felt this exact way. Thanks for being real."

> *One more superhero reference:* Think of the lovable Groot. He says the same three words over and over, but he infuses them with emotion. Even when he's just saying "I am Groot," he connects.

So don't stress about going viral. You're not just trying to show up in someone's feed. You're trying to stick in their *mind*. In the decision-making moments of your Exact Right Customers.

That's the real work of small business marketing. Not just to get seen—but to get *stuck* in someone's memory in the best possible way.

PART II

THE PROCESS

Welcome to Part II of this book—where we stop discussing the problem and start wielding some actual solutions.

If Part I was the superhero origin story, this is the superhero suit-up scene. This is where you start working with a framework that's built specifically for *you*—a small business with a big voice and zero interest in being boring.

CHAPTER 4

Introducing Customer Brandships™

At the heart of this next section is something I hinted at earlier, called **Customer Brandships.** I've illustrated it with a **Venn Diagram** because who doesn't love a good Venn Diagram? And because sometimes the only way to explain something this powerful is with fancy overlapping circles.

Here's how it works:

As we discussed, there are three main challenges every business faces, and should strive to be:

1. **Differentiated** – You can't stand out if you look and sound like everyone else.

2. **Trustworthy** – If they don't trust you, they're less likely to buy from you.

3. **Unforgettable** – If they forget you, it's over. Period.

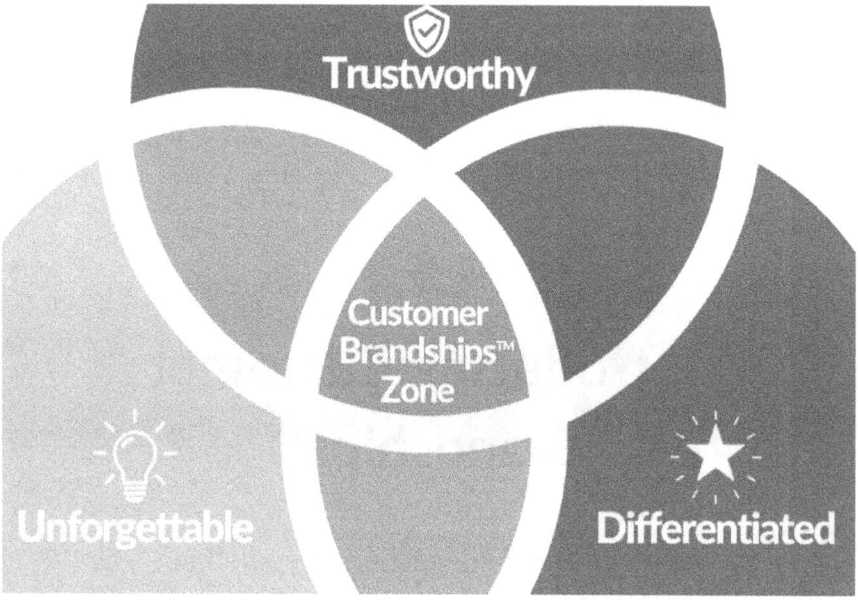

When you consistently show up with these three core traits, you land in what I call the **Customer Brandships™ Zone**—that magic middle where marketing starts to feel less like selling and more like bonding.

But here's where it gets even cooler:

The overlaps between those primary goals create **three secondary superpowers**:

- **Relatable** - When you're both Trustworthy *and* Unforgettable, you become someone your audience sees themselves in.

- **Influential** - When you're both Trustworthy *and* Differentiated, people start repeating your ideas and trusting your lead.
- **Magnetic** - When you're both Differentiated *and* Unforgettable, you don't just attract attention—you pull in loyalty.

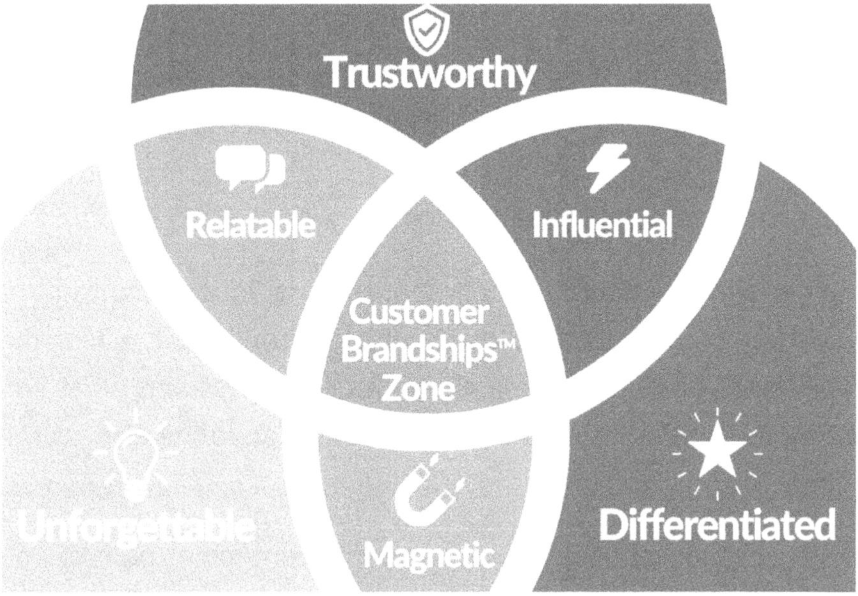

Put all of this together, and you've got a marketing strategy that doesn't require a giant budget or a full-time content team—just clarity, intention, and a little bravery to try something new.

So, in the next six sections, we're going to explore each trait—primary and secondary—and show you exactly how to bring them to life in your business.

Because when you hit the Zone?

People don't just buy from you.
They trust you. They share you. They *remember* you.
That's not just good marketing. That's a superpower.

Primary Trait One – Differentiated

Let's kick off this framework the way every superhero story should: by making sure you don't blend in with the extras.

If people can't tell what makes you different, they'll assume you're the same. Same as the other wellness coach. Same as the other agency. Same as the other "We put people first" business that hasn't returned an email in three weeks.

Being **Differentiated** is not about being louder, fancier, or quirkier for the sake of it. It's about being confidently taking the risk to stand out in talking about your business and what you bring to the table—and how you're unlike anything else on the menu.

Let's get tactical: What makes you different might be *how* you deliver your service. It might be *why* you do it. It might be your values, your tone, your background, your client experience, your spicy opinions, or your approach. It might even be what you *don't* do.

And no, "we care more" doesn't count unless you're willing to show exactly *how* (and it really is 1000% unique).

In fact, here's a quick test. If a competitor could copy and paste your tagline or Instagram bio and no one would notice the difference? You've got a sameness problem, not a marketing problem.

That's your directive to stop being vague and start being *specific*.

- **So instead of saying:**
  "We help businesses grow with proven strategies..."

  Say:
  "We help overlooked small brands outsmart big ones by ditching outdated marketing fluff and getting radically human."

That's a message people can feel. It's clear, it's crisp, and it's not trying to please everyone.

Being **Differentiated** also doesn't mean reinventing the wheel. It means showing your customers that *your* wheel is the exact right wheel for *them*. Your story, your process, your stance—they all add up to a brand nobody else can fake.

Want to see this in action?

- **You're a natural foods store and you say:**
  "You shouldn't need a dictionary to understand the ingredients in your granola."

- You're a creative agency and you say:
  "We specialize in design that makes your audience stop scrolling and start screenshotting."

- **You're a bookkeeper and you say:**
  "We love spreadsheets and hate jargon. You'll get financial clarity without the mumbo-jumbo."

Those aren't elevator pitches. They're truth bombs. And they *work* because they're rooted in something real.

Want help with this part? Visit the Superpower Vault for free resources: www.bit.ly/superpowervault

> *My final superhero reference:* Think of this as your mutant power. You're not just another turtle—you're a ninja! It's time to stop hiding behind a "safe" tagline.

Primary Trait Two – Trustworthy

Next up is **Trustworthy**—because being different is only powerful if people believe what you say.

If Differentiated gets people to notice you, **Trustworthy** makes them stay.

Big brands have beaten the word "trust" to death. They use it like a marketing air freshener—spraying it on everything. "Trust us," they say, as they secretly sell your data or sneakily cut the volume of cereal but keep the box the same size, hoping you won't notice.

Small businesses definitely have the advantage here. We can build trust in real-time, one small moment at a time.

It's not about looking perfect. It's about being *present and honest*—especially when things go sideways.

And yes, the bar is low. A recent Edelman Trust Barometer report found that 76% of people say they're more likely to trust brands that "acknowledge their mistakes in real-time and respond transparently[13]." That's means even when you make a mistake—your superpower is that you can quickly turn that mistake into trust. And the more publicly you share that mistake, the wider the trust net you're casting.

Let's make it real:

- **Instead of: "We're sorry for the inconvenience."**
  Say This: "Yep, we botched that link. Here's the fix—and a little something to say thanks for your patience."
- **Instead of: "We're handling your request."**
  Say this: "Hi [name], we saw your message and we're on it. It might take a little extra time, because our small but mighty team is a bit backlogged, but we'll keep you updated."
- **Instead of: [Radio silence]**
  Say this: "Hey, we didn't mean to ghost you like a bad Prom date! We've been heads-down on some internal stuff, but we're back—and we promise to do better."

---

[13] Source: Edelman, "2025 Trust Barometer," www.edelman.com

These aren't just copy tweaks. They're trust deposits.

And when your customers know you'll show up honestly—even when you mess up? That's when trust gets baked into your brand (kinda like the amazing Challah bread I make once a year).

Want to build trust *before* they even buy? Here's how:

- Show your face. Let them hear your voice.
- Share the "why" behind your mission—not just the features of your products.
- Be honest about who your Exact Right Customers are, and who they aren't.
- Let real customers speak for you.

Here's a stat that proves it matters: According to a 2024 TrustPilot survey, 88% of customers say they're more likely to buy from a brand that shares behind-the-scenes content and shows the human side of the business[14].

Next, we'll dig into Unforgettable—the third core trait in your Brandships triangle. Because even the most trusted brand won't thrive if no one remembers who you are.

---

[14] Source: Lucidpress, "2024 State of Brand Consistency Report," www.lucidpress.com

Primary Trait Three – Unforgettable

Let's talk about the thing most small businesses forget to think about: being **Unforgettable**.

Because if being Differentiated gets you noticed, and being Trustworthy makes you credible, then being **Unforgettable** ensures you're the one people come back to *when it actually matters*—the moment they're ready to buy, refer, or shout you out online.

And in a world where people are hit with over 10,000 brand messages a day, being remembered is the marketing equivalent of having superpowers.

So how do you do it?

Not by being louder. Being **Unforgettable** is about clarity, personality, and emotional impact.

It's the stories you tell. The way you say things. The videos people tell you they remember for months afterward.

Here are a couple more examples for a local natural foods retailer:

- **Instead of:**
  "Healthy food. Local ingredients. Friendly service."

  Say:
  "We're basically your neighborhood farmers market—but indoors, year-round, and no mosquitoes."

- **Instead of:**
  "Wholesome groceries for the whole family."

  Say:
  "We sell stuff your grandma would recognize and your gut will thank you for."

Each line tells the same truth—but it hits differently because it's crafted to stick.

Want proof that this works? A 2024 report by Wistia found that branded content using humor is 2.6 times more likely to be remembered and shared than generic messaging[15].

Being unforgettable means knowing what makes you distinct and expressing it in a way that people can't help but recall. It takes a little bravery at first, but before long, it becomes second nature.

Now let's look at a vet clinic:

- **Spicy take on an industry norm:**
  "If you're only coming in when it's vaccination time, we're missing what really matters: *preventing problems*, not just checking boxes."

---

[15] Source: Wistia, "2024 Brand Video Performance Report," www.wistia.com

- **Quirky metaphor:**
  "Your dog's health is like your phone battery—it doesn't go from 100 to 1% in a day. If she's suddenly acting off, something's been draining her in the background."

- **Emotional moment that makes people feel seen:**
  "We once had a client burst into tears during a nail trim—not because her dog was scared, but because someone finally *listened* to her about his anxiety. That's the kind of vet care we believe in."

- **Sharp, funny honesty:**
  "Look, we know half of you Google symptoms before you call us. We're not mad—but we *are* going to lovingly talk you down from diagnosing your pug with a rare sub-Saharan disease."

Each example says the same thing: We're not like everyone else, and here's why you'll remember us.

Being **Unforgettable** doesn't mean being weird just for the clicks (again, if that's working for you, carry on, my wayward son [bonus points if you're old enough to get that reference]). It means knowing what makes *you* distinct and bravely expressing it in a way that goes against boring industry norms—instilling memories people can't help but recall.

And this one's important: Your message shouldn't sound like a broken record on endless repeat—that will annoy your audience! My own polls from dozens of live audiences get the same results almost every time: we only tolerate the same marketing message two times before getting annoyed. It's about telling your stories in a different way each time, and coming up with new stories to convey what you do, and why.

Next, we'll discuss the secondary traits—where primary traits overlap in the coolest Venn Diagram I've ever created (OK, maybe it's the *only* one I've ever created, but still...).

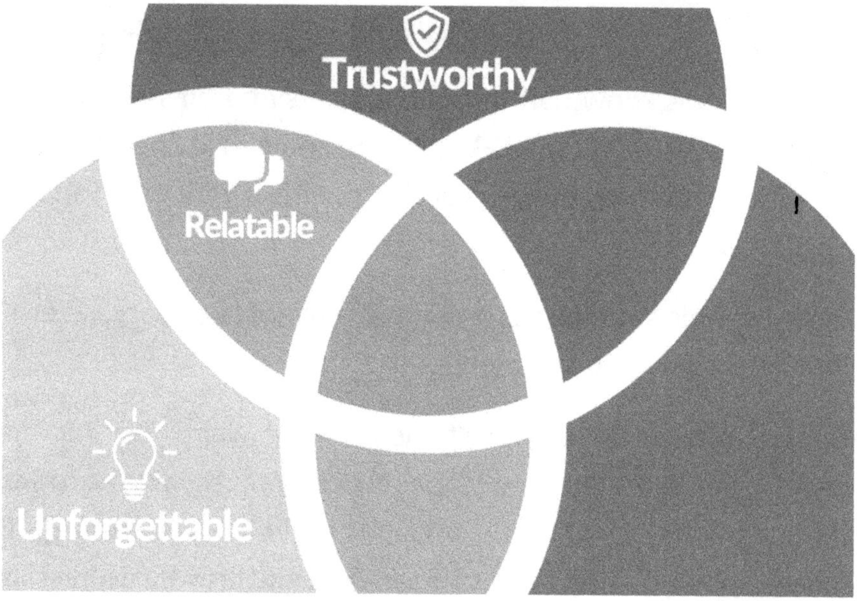

Now onto the Secondary Traits...

Secondary Trait #1 – Relatable

Venn diagram intersection: Trustworthy + Unforgettable = Relatable

You've built credibility (Trustworthy) and you've done it in ways that are truly unique (Differentiated) and sticky (Unforgettable). Now it's time to make people feel like they *know you*—even if they've never met you. That's the magic of being **Relatable**.

Relatable brands make you lean in without realizing it. They talk like real people. They joke about real life. They tell the truth—not the press release version of it. And in doing so, they turn casual browsers into loyal fans.

Because here's what most modern marketing misses: People don't connect with polish. They connect with *familiarity*.

Being **Relatable** isn't about being overshare-y or goofy for the algorithm (unless, as always, if that's your vibe, you do you!). It's about creating that "OMG, same" moment that builds instant connection.

Your audience doesn't need you to impress them—they need you to *understand them*. That's what creates trust and resonance. That's what makes someone think, "Finally... someone who *gets* it." That's being **Relatable**.

A recent brand authenticity report from Stackla found that 88% of consumers say authenticity is a key factor in deciding which brands they support—and 59% say small businesses are more relatable than big brands[16]. That stat? It's not just encouraging—it's your edge.

So let's talk about what **Relatable** actually sounds like.

Say This, Not That:

- **You're a fitness coach. Instead of:**
  "Sign up for my proven transformation system and become your strongest self."

  Say:
  "I used to eat candy bars for dinner and call it self-care. You too? Cool. Let's fix it."

- **You're a copywriter. Instead of:**
  "I help purpose-driven brands clarify their message."

- **Say:**
  "If your 'About Me' page still says 'Coming Soon' six months later... hi. I'm your person."

---

[16] Source: Stackla, "2025 Brand Authenticity Report," www.stackla.com

- **You're a business coach. Instead of:**
  "Unlock your entrepreneurial potential with my 6-step process."

  Say:
  "I once Googled 'what's an LLC' while pitching my first client. If that's you, let's build from there."

- **You're a veterinarian. Instead of:**
  "Expert care for your dog's health needs."

  Say:
  "If your dog panics before you even park, we're the clinic with the good treats and the calming, dog-approved vibes."

- **You're an HVAC company. Instead of:**
  "Reliable heating and cooling solutions for your home."

  Say:
  "We show up on time, don't track mud on your carpet, and explain things without sounding like an instruction manual."

- **You're an auto repair shop. Instead of:**
  "Trusted auto service since 1982."

  Say:
  "We translate weird car noises into plain English—and no, you don't need a new transmission every time."

Relatable doesn't have to mean unprofessional, if that's not your jam. It means understandable. It means *familiar enough to feel safe*. And safe customers are loyal customers.

Relatability also works wonders when you want to educate without lecturing.

Take a dog trainer, for example:

- **Instead of:**
  "Dogs aren't the problem—communication is."

  Say:
  "Your dog isn't trying to ruin your life—he's just fluent in squirrel."

It makes people laugh. But it also lands a real insight in a way they just *get*.

THE SIDEKICK SAYS:

IF SOMEONE'S EVER TAGGED A FRIEND IN ONE OF YOUR POSTS AND SAID, "THIS IS SO YOU," YOU'VE ALREADY NAILED RELATABILITY. DOUBLE DOWN.

And if you're wondering, "But won't being real make me sound less polished?"—yes. That's the point. Because perfect is suspicious. **Relatable** is magnetic.

When was the last time a perfectly filtered and obviously scripted influencer made you *trust* them more? Exactly.

Here's what **Relatable** does in the real world:

- It lowers defenses.
- It earns attention without shouting.
- It turns lurkers into loyalists.
- It creates content that feels like a conversation, not a pitch.

And when your brand gets that real, people stop comparing you to your competition and start inviting you into their world. You don't need to market *at* them—you're already talking *with* them.

Secondary Trait #2 – Influential

Venn diagram intersection: Trustworthy + Differentiated = Influential

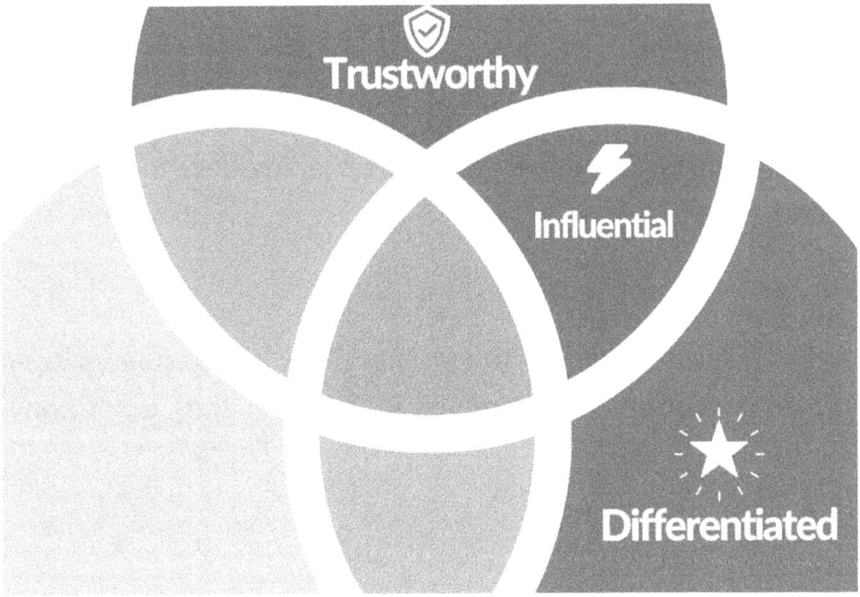

Let's talk about the kind of power that doesn't require a blue checkmark, a best-selling book, or a 10K-person email list.
Let's talk about being **Influential**. It's when people don't just notice what you say—they start *quoting* it.

They forward your emails. They reference your posts at the dinner table. They say things like, "I saw something you posted the other day and haven't stopped thinking about it."

That's **Influential**. And it's not magic. It's marketing with integrity, clarity, and just the right amount of you.

Big brands have scale. You have beliefs. And belief is what actually moves people.

Influence isn't about being the loudest—it's about saying something that *matters* in a way that sticks.

How It Works

When your audience knows what you stand for—and they trust you enough to believe it—you start shaping how they see the world.

And that's the game-changer.

A 2024 Nielsen report found that **92% of consumers trust recommendations from individuals—even if they don't know**

them—over brand ads[17]. So the "influencer" with 3,000 real-life fans who believe in her? More powerful than the Fortune 500 with a full-page ad today.

Say This, Not That:

- **You're a financial coach. Instead of:**
  "Let's unlock your financial potential."

  Say:
  "I don't believe budgets are about restriction—they're about freedom."

- **You're a bakery. Instead of:**
  "Baked fresh daily with quality ingredients."

  Say:
  "We think birthdays deserve real butter, not mass-produced frosting."

- **You're a dog trainer. Instead of:**
  "Effective training solutions for every breed."

  Say:
  "Your dog isn't the problem—your roommate's habits are."

---

[17] Nielsen, "2024 Consumer Trust Index," www.nielsen.com

Now let's go deeper:

- **You're a natural foods store. Instead of:**
  "Clean ingredients for a healthy life."

  Say:
  "If your almond milk has 19 ingredients on the label, we're not stocking it."

- **You're a dentist. Instead of:**
  "Trusted dental care in your community."

  Say:
  "We're not judging your floss game—we're just here to help you keep your teeth when you're 80."

- **You're a business consultant. Instead of:**
  "I help brands scale sustainably."

  Say:
  "If 'growth' means your team's in therapy and you hate your business, it's not success. Let's rethink what scaling looks like."

Case in Point: Micro-Messages with Macro Impact

Influence builds through patterns—those little phrases you repeat because they're *true*, not just catchy. Those emotionally sticky ideas become part of your brand's DNA. They help customers align with you on a belief level.

Let's say you're a marketing coach and your line is:

"People don't want to be pitched. They want to be understood."

Suddenly, it's not just a sentence—it's something that resonates with the right people. Maybe even quote.

That's how influence happens.

THE SIDEKICK SAYS:

IF SOMEONE CAN'T SUMMARIZE YOUR POINT OF VIEW IN ONE SENTENCE, YOU'RE NOT BEING INFLUENTIAL—YOU'RE BEING VAGUE. SHARPEN YOUR LINE. THEN REPEAT IT—CREATIVELY.

Why It Works

When people trust you, and your message sticks, they're far more likely to adopt your perspective and share it. This is where real marketing impact begins—not with clicks, but with *conversion of thought*.

That's the power of being influential. You become someone your audience doesn't just listen to... they *align* with.

You're the brand they reference when defending a point. The one they forward to a friend. The one they think of when a problem pops up.

You're not just relevant—you're remembered, respected, and referred.

Coming up next: Trait Six — Magnetic—because nothing's better than customers who **stick around** (see what I did there?).

Secondary Trait #3 — Magnetic

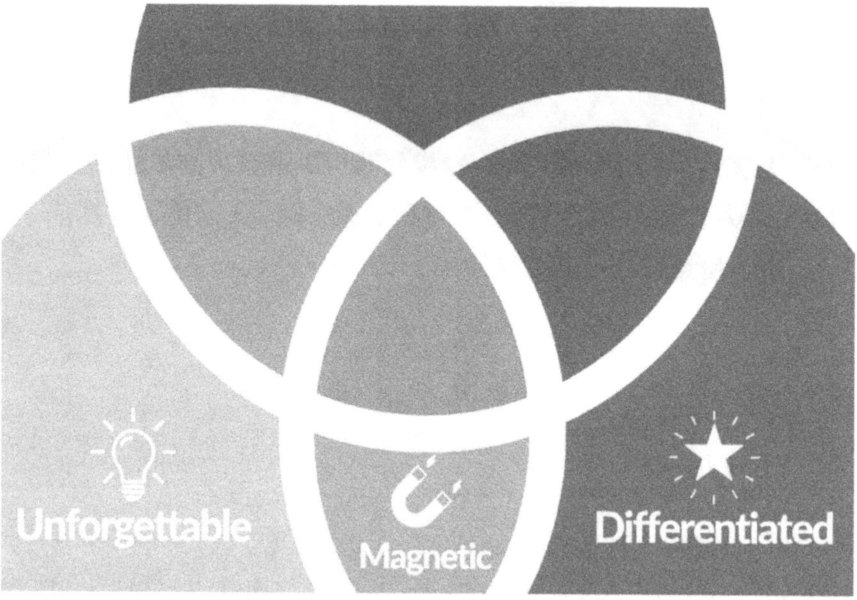

Venn diagram intersection: Unforgettable + Differentiated = Magnetic

Some brands make you lean in without even realizing it.

You weren't planning to read the whole post, watch the whole video, or forward that email to your best friend—but here you are.

That's **magnetism**. And it's not luck or lighting. It's the natural result of a brand being both *different* and *unforgettable*.

When people trust you and can tell you're not like everyone else, they're drawn in—without needing to be bribed, tricked, or bombarded.

That's the difference between a brand that's *pulling* (like a magnet) vs. a brand that's *pushing*.

What Makes a Brand Magnetic?

It's not shenanigans, tomfoolery, or even hijinks (nobody uses these amazing words enough anymore). As my GenZ daughter would say, "*It's giving*: I don't know why, but I want to keep listening."

You don't need to go viral to be magnetic. You just need to be consistent enough in your personality and presence that people start saying:

"You've gotta check this out—it's so you."

That's magnetism.

Say This, Not That:

- **You're a candle maker. Instead of:**
  "Hand-poured candles for every mood."

Say:
"We make candles for people who'd rather cancel the dinner party and stay home with a blanket and a book."

Now remix it:

"Our candles smell like someone actually thought about your vibe."
"This one's called 'Not Today, Chaos'—it smells like calm, coffee, and boundaries."
"Burn if overstimulated, overcommitted, or over everyone."

You're not just selling wax—you're calling your exact right people.

The Magnetic Advantage

People love discovering something that feels like it was made *just for them*. They love finding the thing that gets them before they even had words for what they needed.

Magnetic brands:

- Call out the audience's identity
- Name the deeper desire
- Show up with a vibe no one else does

That's what you're doing when you marry your *differentiation* with *being unforgettable.*

You become someone's favorite *not because you pushed*—but because you *resonated.*

A Fictional Case Study: The Fruitery Juicery

Let's say you're a small cold-pressed juice bar in Asheville called **The Fruitery Juicery**.

You've got a small storefront, an edgy aesthetic, and a mission to make wellness weird in the best way.

Your competitors are saying:

"Fresh. Local. Organic."

You're saying:

"Gut-friendly juice for people who still eat Hot Cheetos."

And your customers? They're *telling their friends* about you—not just because the product's great, but because the *brand makes them feel seen.*

That's magnetism. People want to bring others into the feeling.

Why Big Brands Can't Fake This

Big brands try to be magnetic by pretending they're quirky, cool, or "just like you." But they get awkward about it. They use Gen Z slang like a substitute teacher (I see my own irony, since I just quoted my GenZ kid). They overcorrect with TikTok trends they don't understand. They drop into your inbox with lines like:

"Hey bestie! 15% off ends soon!" And consumers sniff out the chicanery and the flimflam instantly.

You? You don't have to pretend. Your weird is real. Your voice is yours. Your edge is earned. Which means you can be magnetic without being manufactured. You just have to give yourself permission to do it, if you haven't already.

THE SIDEKICK SAYS:

THE EASIEST WAY TO BE MAGNETIC? STOP DILUTING WHAT MAKES YOU DIFFERENT. BE WEIRDER. BE BOLDER. BE MORE YOU.

Stat Check

A recent Stackla report found that 88% of consumers say authenticity influences which brands they support, and 59% say small businesses are more relatable than big brands[18].

Magnetism starts with being real—then turned up just enough to cut through the noise.

Your brand doesn't need to be "for everyone." It needs to be unforgettable to *your people*. Would you rather be overly vanilla

---

[18] Stackla, "2025 Brand Authenticity Report," www.stackla.com

and not really magnetic to everyone, or attract ridiculously loyal fans who become like ambassadors of your awesomeness? If you choose vanilla, get comfortable with the fact that you'll likely never reach a massive audience because you don't stand for something that's magnetic. If you choose the latter, though, get comfortable letting go of the customers who don't get it, to make room for the raving fans who will.

Coming up next: how all six traits power the ultimate goal—Customer Brandships™.

Wrapping It Up: Building in the Brandships™ Zone

Let's zoom out and look at what you just accomplished.

You didn't just learn six marketing traits. You unlocked the foundation of building *Customer Brandships™*—those rare, almost friendship-like relationships your audience forms with your brand when it feels *real*, *aligned*, and *undeniably unforgettable*.

This framework isn't just a way to market. It's a way to **matter**.

Because here's the reality: Marketing that's rooted in truth, clarity, and character doesn't just convert—it compounds over time.
It snowballs into brand loyalty. It earns referrals without asking. It builds customer relationships that can outlast recessions, rebrands, price increases, and even relocation.

Let's take one final lap around each trait—not to recap, but to reinforce.

Recapping the Six Traits That Power Real Connection

1. Trustworthy

This isn't about plastering "we care" on a banner. It's about doing what you say, fixing what you break, and being *present*—even when it's inconvenient.

> *Trust is fragile—but when it's real, it becomes your strongest referral engine.*

2. Differentiated

Differentiated brands don't try to please everyone. They get clear on their edge, own their lane, and show up boldly enough that the *right* people find them faster.

> *It's the difference between, "Oh, another wellness coach," and, "Wait, she works only with chronically tired women who don't trust traditional medicine anymore? Yes please." Which one do you think grows faster in a crowded market?*

3. Unforgettable

Unforgettable brands don't just "build awareness"—they build emotion. They use language, visuals, micro-stories, and tone that make people *feel* something—and remember you because of it.

> *This is where your quirks shine. Your values **and** your vibe become unmistakable.*

4. Influential

Influential brands don't follow trends—they start conversations. They put a stake in the ground and invite people to join them.

> *That's you stepping into your voice and truly owning your niche. It's being one in a million vs. one of a million.*

5. Relatable

Relatable brands make customers laugh, nod, or say, "Oh thank *God*, I thought I was the only one."

> *This is the brand that shares the behind-the-scenes mess, admits when it's figuring things out, and sounds more like a best friend than a boardroom.*

6. Magnetic

Magnetic brands don't chase—they attract. They don't have to explain themselves over and over because their vibe is clear, consistent, and aligned with their values.

> *This is the brand people talk about at brunch. The one their friend DMs them because "this just feels like you."*

This Is Your Zone

When all six traits are in play, you're not just doing marketing. You're *creating connection.* You're operating in the **Customer Brandships™ Zone**—and that's where the magic lives.

And no, you don't have to nail all six traits perfectly every day. That's not the point.

The point is that *now you know what to aim for.* Now you've got a filter for every message you send, every touchpoint you create, every decision you make (every cake you bake...Thanks, Sting).

PART III

THE TOOLS

Alrighty—so now what?

We've talked about the why, the what, the "oh wow, that's why that wasn't working." But what do you actually *do* with all this?

You take it to the places where your prospects' ears and eyeballs hang out. I'm talking: your website, emails, chalkboard sign, that voicemail message you recorded three years ago and need to update. All the things, including the biggest one of them all: social media.

Part III is about figuring out the marketing tools that work for you and showcase your business in the best possible way to your customers.

Let's figure out what tools make sense for *you*, without making it a full-time job or hiring a branding agency. Let's make sure you have what you need to show up where, when, and how you need to. Ready? Let's go tool shopping.

CHAPTER 5

Social Media Without the Flimflam

The Great Misunderstanding

Confession time...I used to think I had to be *everywhere* on social media to be taken seriously. ALL the platforms. All the time. I tried it—Facebook, LinkedIn, Instagram, Twitter (before it got weird), even TikTok for a hot second.

I spent way too long thinking I just wasn't doing it right. That if I could just crack the "viral" code, the magic would happen. Spoiler: it didn't.

And honestly, I got tired. It felt like every time I figured out what worked, the algorithm would change (Can we not do that? Looking at you, Zuckerberg, et al).

The worst part? I was so focused on getting seen by *everyone*, I forgot my own advice--that I wasn't trying to sell to everyone. I was trying to be remembered by the right ones. The real people who might actually hire me. And those people? They're mainly on two platforms for me, so that's where I focus my time and energy now.

I don't need to be everywhere. I just need to matter *where they are.*

Why You Can't Just Measure Likes & Follows

Just because people aren't following, liking, or commenting doesn't mean they're not paying attention. Most people are lurkers. They scroll, they watch, they absorb—and they never so much as double-tap. But then one day they show up in your inbox or make an appointment and say, "I've been following you for a while." And you're thinking... *Really? Because you've literally never engaged with a single thing I've posted.*

That's why you can't measure your social media success solely on likes or shares. Vanity metrics are loud—but not always honest. The real magic is happening behind the scenes. It's in the quiet brand awareness. The steady trust-building. The moment someone fills out your intake form and selects "Instagram" as how they found you—even though you didn't see a single comment from them.

Social is a long game, so just keep showing up. You can't post for a week or two and decide it's not working for you.

Why Quality is Better than Quantity (For Most of Us)

It's hard to accept that going viral isn't the goal for most small businesses. Sure, if you have a product and want to sell a million of them, reach matters more than loyalty. In that case, go on Shark Tank! But if you're a local or regional business, a service business, an industry-specific business, or a niche business, massive reach isn't the goal.

Contradiction Alert! I know I've shared an example or two of small business owners getting thousands of likes on a video, and I've said, "Isn't that great?" I'm not saying it isn't. It's fantastic when it happens, because the platform's algorithm shares popular videos even more. Nevertheless, the 100 likes you get from your Exact Right Customers often have more business impact than 50,000 random likes or views from the general public. It all comes down to your business model, what you're selling, and where your customers' eyeballs hang out.

A financial planner in Iowa doesn't need national visibility, unless she wants to become a national expert. She needs to matter where her prospects are, which is likely Facebook if they're GenX or older, or Instagram if they're younger.

My friend, professional speaker Dr. Janel Anderson, has a niche speaking to large tech companies and IT leaders, including, but not limited to, people designing UX. She doesn't need massive reach on TikTok; she needs targeted visibility to her prospects, who can bc found on LinkedIn.

Viral doesn't mean diddly if it's to the wrong crowd. I'd rather be seen by 50 ideal prospects who actually want to hire me to speak or consult, vs. the feel-good virality of a million random viewers. Every. Damn. Time.

It took me too long to figure that out. But once I did, things got way simpler—and way better. I started posting less, but connecting more. I stopped chasing likes and started responding better to DMs. I stopped trying to impress, and just started being present.

I narrowed down the platforms that work for me from six down to just two. That's where my prospects hang out. It's resulted in less stress for me, less busywork for my assistant, and way better results.

> *I want you to be one IN a million, rather than one OF a million, to the specific audience you want to serve.*

So if you're feeling burnt out by social, like it's a second job you never signed up for... I get it. Fully. And it doesn't have to be that way.

Let's talk about how to make this feel doable again. Maybe even (dare I say it?) enjoyable.

Choosing the Right Platform(s) for You

Once you give yourself permission to stop being everywhere, everything changes. I firmly believe it's better to go all-in and consistent on a couple platforms, than to go wide and thin on all of them.

Your mission? Pick 1–2 platforms and show up in a way that actually suits you and reaches your audience.

How to choose:

1. **Audience Whereabouts**
   Over 90% of small businesses now use social media, and 78% of consumers research brands there before buying[19]. Meet them where their eyeballs are!

2. **Consistency Without Burnout**
   Choose formats that fit in your chosen rhythm (i.e. daily, weekly). It's better to post once a week consistently than to go full bore, posting daily for a while, then posting nothing for days or weeks on end (ask me how I know).

Think of platforms as tools in your utility belt. You don't need them all—just the useful ones where you can deliver your best work consistently.

[19] Synup, "Social Media Marketing Statistics 2025" www.synup.com

Platform Comparison Table (from ChatGPT)

Platform	Strengths	Weaknesses	Audience Profile
Instagram	Highly visual, strong Stories & Reels	Highly competitive, time-intensive	18–44, image-driven viewers
Facebook	Great for local business & communities	Low organic reach	35–65+, community-focused
LinkedIn	Professional network, B2B-friendly	Can feel formal and slow-growing	30–55, business professionals
TikTok	High engagement, fast learning	Trend-centric, requires frequent content	16–35, casual creators
YouTube	Long-form, evergreen content	Higher production demands	Wide-ranging knowledge seekers
BlueSky	Alternative to TikTok	smaller reach but growing	25–55, left-leaning creators, journalists leaving TikTok
Pinterest	Visual search, tutorial-oriented	More niche, lower everyday engagement	25–44, DIY and lifestyle
Substack	Hot publishing platform for newsletters & blogs	Building audience takes time	28–55, educated, independent thinkers, experts,

Reddit	High-trust communities, great for word-of-mouth	Crowd can be brutal if you're salesy. Has to feel organic to the conversation at hand.	20–45, curious minds, hobbyists, researchers, skeptics
Threads	Quick conversational exchanges, alternative to X.	Still growing, less reach right now	Younger, text-heavy users
"X"	I am deliberately excluding X because I am biased against it and think it's dumbed down now. Thanks, Elon. - Shawna		

Platform Reference Guide

Instagram

This is your visual playground. Reels, Stories, behind-the-scenes—it's all fair game. But don't worry about looking perfect—that's for a niche group who likes to spend hours on the beach, not swimming, but posing and editing. Just show up real. The more "you" it feels, the more it lands. You can edit to add flair, but too much can take away its humanity and authenticity. Always remember to include captions for both accessibility and those who need to keep their devices muted.

Facebook

Still solid for local business and building community. Don't expect fireworks from your business page alone. Use your personal page (you can post things for customers in Public mode, and keep your friend posts just for Friends). Use

Groups—even create your own, but make sure it gives value. Post longer storytelling, real photos, and short videos. Go Live and talk to people like you're sitting across from them. That's where the magic is.

LinkedIn

It's not just for resumes anymore. Thoughtful posts, lessons learned, client wins, even your failures—people want it. And they'll actually read it, especially when it sounds like you, not a ChatGPT-derived press release. Use the Newsletter feature. Try going Live. Two friends of mine do a live broadcast every Saturday morning on LinkedIn, and have enjoyed huge success with that.

TikTok

Trends are fun, but not required. Teach something. Say something honest. Be weird and fun, if that's your thing. Low-gloss = high trust here. Just be consistent and show up. NOTE: if you're creating for TikTok, it's easy to share the same video on YouTube Shorts.

YouTube

Great if you've got how-tos, behind-the-scenes, or anything people might search for later. Treat it like a content library, not a party. It's slower, but the payoff sticks around, so evergreen content is especially good here. Evergreen refers to content that is relevant for a long time, because you don't mention a specific date, season, upcoming promotion, etc. NOTE: if you're creating for YouTube Shorts, it's easy to share the same video on TikTok (but only do this if your audience hangs out on TikTok. Otherwise, don't bother. Just because it's easy doesn't mean it's purposeful).

Bluesky

Best if you're into community-building and want to hang with early adopters. It's like Twitter's cooler cousin who left the party early to build something better. The vibe is more thoughtful, less chaotic and oppositional. Still small, still growing, but great for experimenting and having real conversations. Not a place for blasting promos—think personality over pitch.

Pinterest

Think evergreen here, as well. How-to guides, visual tips, blog post promos. Great for anything people search for while planning. Make it visually appealing and useful.

Substack

You've got thoughts and love to write? Good. Write them. Substack is the newer kid on the block, and gives you a space to go deep and build trust over time.

Reddit

Zero tolerance for fake. Be real, be useful, be generous. Answer questions, share advice, and let the relationship build without selling.

Threads

Low pressure, fast posting. A place to test an idea, share a quick thought, or engage in a convo without needing to polish it up.

X (formerly Twitter)

OK, ok, I'll include it. Some people love it for short-form ideas, strong opinions, and sharing links. If you're already there, keep the momentum going. If not, don't bother. Just don't expect deep connection—it's more fly-by.

Stats to Encourage You to Do More Video

- **Video is far more effective at retaining your message.** Recent studies showed viewers remember **95%** of a message when watched via video, compared to just **10%** when read in text[20].
- 85% of marketers planned to increase video budgets in 2025[21].

NOTE to the video-phobes: If doing videos feels totally uncomfortable, I get it. But I highly encourage you to get comfortable (especially with selfie videos), because it's the most

---

[20] www.sproutsocial.com/insights/social-media-video-statistics/

[21] Dash, "Video Marketing Statistics 2025" — www.dash.app

humanizing, trust-building format out there. Repetition is what gets you comfortable, so just eat the frog, as they say. Poor frog.

Time-Saving Tip: Repurpose, Repurpose, Repurpose!

Let's say you're a REALTOR® who created a 7-minute selfie video titled *"Top 8 Suggestions to Increase Your Home's Selling Price"*. Here are 11 different ways to repurpose that one asset:

1. **Edit it into 8 Reels/Shorts** - Each one covers one tip on Instagram or Facebook
2. **Create a "Top 3" Highlights Reel** - A 60-second roundup of the most high-impact suggestions.
3. **Transcribe into a Blog Post** - Just add a visual or two and share on your website or put a link on any platform.
4. **Upload the blog post into ChatGPT** and ask it to create a different social media post for each tip.
5. **Turn into a Carousel for Instagram or LinkedIn** - Each slide highlights one tip with a visual and takeaway. Easy-peasy on Canva.
6. **Email Newsletter Feature** - Makes a great "how-to" guide for sellers.
7. **Create a Downloadable Tip Sheet** - Offer a printable version of the tips as a free lead magnet on your website and social media, and as a hand-out at open houses.

8. **Use as Talking Points for a Facebook Live Q&A** - Invite questions around home value strategies.
9. **Quote Graphics for Social** - Turn client-friendly tips into branded quote visuals.
10. **Create a Postcard** - Share the tips in a mailer or trade show
11. **Reshare on a Schedule** If your video is evergreen, you can repurpose it, and all the assets that came from it, on a schedule that makes sense. In this case, I would recommend this content to be re-shared no more than every 4-6 weeks.

A.I.: Hello, Elephant (or Should I Say Robot) in the Room!

I'd be remiss (or so 2019) if I didn't talk about A.I. It's not a social media platform, but it's an amazing tool that can help you leverage your platforms with greater consistency, without ever running out of ideas for content.

Here's a summary on how best to use ChatGPT, written by ChatGPT:

"Yes, I can help you write content. No, it shouldn't sound like a robot. And no, it's not cheating. It's a tool—like Canva, or email, or that one employee who *actually* knows how the printer works. The pros? It's fast. It's idea-generating gold. It can break writer's block in less time than it takes you to microwave leftovers. But the downside? If you copy-paste the output without adding your own seasoning, it'll sound like you outsourced your brand voice to an AI intern with a thesaurus addiction."

Chad (the name of my ChatGPT) went on to share these tips:

1. **Start with your own voice.** Before you ask ChatGPT to write anything, give it a sample of your real tone and style. A social post. An email. Something you actually wrote. Ask it to match *that* tone. (Bonus tip: tell it what *not* to do. Say, "Don't sound corporate or fluffy." You'll thank me.)

2. **Use it like a brainstorm partner, not a ghostwriter.** Ask for ideas. Headlines. Trends. First drafts. But always—*always*—rewrite to sound like you. If you wouldn't say it out loud at a backyard BBQ, rewrite it.

3. **Keep the "you-ness."** Add in your stories, your weird metaphors, your offbeat humor. AI can't replicate your lived experience or your personality.

IMPORTANT!

OK, enough from Chad. I'm back. When using A.I., for the love of pizza and all that is holy, please train it to know who your customers are, and to use your tone and voice. You can upload other things you've written so it doesn't spit out boring corporate language. Don't give up all of your you-ness for convenience!

Here's a reminder to check out the free Superpower Vault I built for you, which will have the latest marketing resources and tools at your disposal. A.I. is evolving so quickly, if I get too specific here, it'll be outdated in three months!

www.bit.ly/superpowervault or go here:

Summary

- You only need **1–2 platforms** that align with your audience and strengths.
- **90%** of small businesses use social media; most marketers are ramping up video spend.
- Repurpose assets strategically to extend reach without investing a lot of time.
- Use A.I. as a tool if you want to, but don't give it the reins.

Action Steps

1. Choose one or two platforms based on where your audience is and what format you enjoy.

2. Create an original asset (e.g., video or post) this week.
3. Try to repurpose it into at least three different formats to use across your chosen platforms.

THE SIDEKICK SAYS:

IT ISN'T ABOUT AMASSING EVERY TOOL—IT'S ABOUT MASTERING THE ONES IN YOUR BELT. PRIORITIZE QUALITY OVER QUANTITY, CONSISTENCY OVER OVERWHELM, AND STRATEGY OVER SCATTER. YOU'LL BE MORE EFFECTIVE—AND WAY LESS BURNT OUT.

Human Over Hype

Glossy filters and perfectly scripted content don't win hearts anymore—people do. Years ago, I did what many speakers have done: I hired a well-known fancy video editor to create a scripted demo reel of me speaking against a green screen. He then dropped in backgrounds that were very polished, sprinkled in footage of beautiful people doing 'marketing things' in pretty boardrooms. And it was...perfect. Months later? The number of views were...meh. I realized I had totally missed the mark, and that my audience had evolved beyond glossy, corporate perfection.

So I scrapped the video and started at square one. Real footage of me on stages big and small, some beautiful and some plain, with footage of my actual audiences reacting to my speeches. We still made it nicely edited together, added music, and voila! So much more "me," especially with the wacky outtakes at the end, which no other speaker does, to my knowledge. Check it out on my home page, www.shawnasuckow.com.

What's even more "me" is when I film my video tips directly into my phone with no script. Just me in my office, or sometimes in my car, or on a walk, sharing my thoughts and suggestions. I don't add music or my logo to those. I just share them as-is but with captions.

I'm not saying don't ever use an editor or go a step further than a raw selfie video. Know your audience and make sure the scripting and editing flair are kept at a minimum.

It takes time for some people to be comfortable enough to go 'off-script', I realize. But with repetition, you'll get far more comfortable and conversational, which is when the magic really happens. My edited demo reel lives on my website, and pinned on my LinkedIn profile. The conversational, casual videos are what I share regularly on my chosen channels.

Here's an example:

Say you need to figure out how to grow a container garden. You go on YouTube and search for videos. An array of suggested videos comes up. Amongst them all, you see polished ones with graphically designed thumbnails (the YouTube equivalent of an album cover). You see sponsored ones. You see videos obviously pitching a product like fertilizer.

Then you see a video of a woman standing on a deck surrounded by 20 different potted veggies. Which video do you trust? I choose the one who looks like a regular person who's a true expert. Who seems like she's not trying to sell me anything, and not trying to be clickbait.

Not long ago, the videos getting the most attention were the ones with the most polished thumbnails, the best graphics, and the most clickbait-y headline screaming something at you like: "If you grow tomatoes like this, everyone you know will DIE!" OK, that might be a bit of an extreme example, but you know clickbait a mile away today when you see it. We all do.

Today, we all have trust issues, as I covered earlier in the book. We no longer want polish, perfection, and shock factor headlines. We want what's real, low-key, helpful, and honest.

That's the vibe you should go for. Less hawking goods, more helping solve pain points.

Why Behind-the-Scenes Content Wins Now

Algorithms today reward *authenticity*. According to Sprout Social, **48% of consumers interact with brands more often now** because they crave transparency[22]. If that number seems low to you, remember all the lurkers who don't interact. And behind-the-scenes content often sparks exactly that—everyone loves a peek behind the curtain.

Showing your real self—your face, your quirks, your voice—builds trust. It's hard not to feel connected when someone's recording in their messy kitchen or talking through their "oops" moments.

Back when I was a corporate meeting planner a million years ago, I remember two very different hotel sales experiences. Both were being remodeled when I toured them.

One of the hotels took me in a hardhat behind the plastic curtain. The other one kept me in a conference room and showed me posters of what the finished product would look like.

I never forgot the hotel who took me behind the scenes. It was The Rio Hotel in Las Vegas. I couldn't tell you the name of the other hotel. Which experience do you think I raved about on social media? The messy, dusty, behind-the-scenes one! Why? Because I got to see something most people didn't.

---

[22] Sprout Social, *80+ Must-Know Social Media Marketing Statistics for 2025*: www.sproutsocial.com

These moments tap into something deeper: people *relate* to the journey, not just the end product. Show your social media audience both!

Here are some B2B examples for companies that many don't see as "sexy" or interesting, to show you that it can be done:

1. **Food Packaging Company**
   Instead of the too-perfect shots of your perfectly labeled product on a grocery shelf, humanize your operation by showing the early-morning crew, the test runs that didn't seal quite right, the high-five when you finally nailed the design that keeps chips crispy *and* customers happy. Let people see the care, not just the carton. That's what turns you from "supplier" to "partner."

2. **Commercial Printer**
   Everyone shows off the glossy finished product. Yawn. Show the machine jamming, the ink-stained hands, the pages that didn't print correctly. Let people feel the real care—and the chaos—that goes into what you do. That's what makes them want *you*, not just "a printer."

3. **Logistics Management Firm**
   Skip the photo of trucks lined up in perfect formation.
   Show the controlled chaos: the 2 a.m. reroute that saved a client's deadline, the dispatcher's victory dance when every pallet arrives on time, the whiteboard of arrows and scribbles that somehow makes sense to your team. When

people see your problem-solving in motion, they stop viewing you as "shipping"—and start seeing you as the heartbeat of their business.

Why Your Face (and Your Team's) Matters

Video posts where you or team members appear get significantly more engagement. HubSpot reported **video posts on LinkedIn generate three times more engagement** than text-only ones[23]. Even on Instagram and TikTok, human faces boost comments, saves, and shares. The algorithm notices.

Data that proves it

- Behind-the-scenes and interactive videos drive engagement in 2025[24].
- Social videos are shared 12x more often than text and images, and are viewed 48% more[25].

---

[23] HubSpot, *45 Video Marketing Statistics for 2025* blog.hubspot.com

[24] Delivered Social, *What Works for Social Media Engagement in 2025* www.deliveredsocial.com

[25] Gudsho (citing Sprout Social), *40+ Must-Know Video Marketing Statistics for 2025* – www.gudsho.com

It's simple math: humans connect with humans. When you bring your real self—no filters—you become visible, unforgettable, and trusted.

Summary

- Real, low-gloss content outperforms polished, scripted posts.
- Consumers crave transparency.
- Video featuring real people drives more engagement.
- Video is shared more and viewed more than other formats.

Action Steps

1. Film one behind-the-scenes video this week—no script, no pressure.
2. Post a short "oops" clip to show your human side.
3. Start showing up on camera regularly—even 30 seconds for Stories or Reels counts.

THE SIDEKICK SAYS:

YOU DON'T NEED A HOLLYWOOD CREW TO CONNECT ON CAMERA—JUST YOUR FACE, YOUR STORY, AND THE COURAGE TO BE REAL. THAT'S THE REAL SUPERPOWER.

Social Ads That Don't Feel Like Snake Oil

Let's talk about paid social. I know, I know—your eye might already be twitching. Social media ads can feel like a rigged game. You boost a post, sprinkle in $50, and what do you get? Zilch.

But social ads absolutely can work. Most small businesses are just playing by rules that no longer apply, or never worked in the first place.

Let's talk about it. Because if you do this right, your ads can actually *build trust*. Yes, really.

What's Out (And Honestly, Has Been for a While)

- **Overly polished videos** with royalty-free music and corporate vibes. Customers can smell that from three scrolls away.

- **Overtly salesy copy.** "LIMITED TIME OFFER" feels less like urgency and more like a red flag.
- Stock photos of perfect people laughing around a perfect table over a perfect meal. Just... no.
- Audience targeting that's as broad as "people who breathe."

This isn't 2019 and you're not trying to win with fake urgency (hurry, this offer ends soon!), and obviously fake scarcity (I only have three more slots left for new clients!). You're a real business, run by real humans. That's the superpower.

The New Playbook: Ads That Feel Like Conversations

Social ads that actually work today do three things really well:

1. **They look native to the feed.** Meaning: they don't scream "ad." They look and feel like posts a friend would make on that same platform.
2. **They focus on relevance over reach.** Small, strategic targeting beats throwing spaghetti at Zuckerberg's proverbial wall.
3. **They spark trust before the click.** The ad itself should offer a micro-story—an insight, a chuckle, a moment of realness.
4. **There's no cheesy Call to Action.** 'Call Today!' doesn't subconsciously make people want to drop everything and call you. They will if and when they feel like it.

In short: *stop trying to be persuasive or pitchy*. Start trying to be useful, or real, or both.

Ad Types That Are Working Right Now (Especially for Small Biz)

1. **The Selfie-Style Video Ad**
   You already know I'm a fan of this marketing tool. These ads *consistently* outperform studio-shot content because they feel unscripted and real. Your dog barking in the background? Leave it in!

2. **The Tip Post**
   Share something your customer didn't know but should. "Most people waste money on [X] because they didn't know [Y]." Helpful = Unforgettable.

3. **The "Peek Behind the Scenes" Video Ad**
   Show how something's made, or a day in the life at your business. There's a young, local painter whose video ads I see on Facebook. He's standing in a room that's mid-way through painting, with visible ladders and drop cloths. Not a room that's done and perfect. His competitors only share the "after" photos and boring facts like 'free estimates' and 'we're insured.'

4. **The Personal Story Post**
   Tell a short story from your journey, your clients, or your process that ties into what you do. Add a small, friendly call

to action like "Want help with this? Message me." Notice I didn't say 'message us.'

5. **The Local Legend Ad**
   These work like crazy for brick-and-mortar. Highlight a well-known customer, tag them, and watch your ad feel like it belongs in the neighborhood. (Because it does.)

Targeting Tip: Go Narrow or Go Home

The most successful social ads today aren't casting wide nets—they're laser focused. That means:

- Retargeting people who've visited your site in a non-creepy way
- Creating custom audiences from your email list
- Targeting lookalikes of *actual customers*, not just your competitors' followers

Also, don't forget: more platforms are shifting toward AI-assisted targeting. That means your **creative matters more than ever**. It has to *land*. If it doesn't, no amount of ad budget will save it.

Chapter Summary

- Social media isn't about being everywhere—it's about being *yourself* somewhere that matters.

- Content that connects starts with conversation, not performance. Talk like a human, not a pitch deck.
- Consistency isn't only about frequency—it's about reliability. Show up on your own rhythm, not the algorithm's (see what I did there?).
- **The best ads don't look like ads.** They look like a helpful, real person talking to another real person.
- **Posting just to post is digital noise.** Say something that matters or skip it. Consistency is better than silence, but even silence is better than B.S.

⚡ Action Steps

1. **Pick Your Rhythm.**
   Decide how often you can show up *well*. Whether it's once a week or three times, commit to it like it's your Tuesday Taco Night. Better yet, film a video during Tuesday Taco Night each week, where you're talking about something totally unrelated to tacos, but it forms your recognizable weekly backdrop.
2. **Create a Content Stash.**
   Jot down 10 go-to content ideas (use the list in your free Superpower Vault at www.shawnasuckow.com/vault).

3. **Film One Selfie-Style Video Ad.**
   No scripts, no polish. Just you, a real moment, and something helpful to say. Post it as an ad—or just post it.

4. **Boost a Post.**
   Use a post that already did well and run it as an ad to a specific audience. No selling. Just connection.

5. **Audit Your Voice.**
   Does your content sound like you—or a webinar robot? Rewrite one piece of recent content in your real voice and compare.

6. **Batch Ideas, Not Pressure.**
   Spend five minutes once a week figuring out content ideas.

THE SIDEKICK SAYS:

IF YOUR CONTENT MAKES YOU CRINGE, YOUR AUDIENCE PROBABLY AGREES. REMEMBER, SAY IT LIKE YOU'D SAY IT TO YOUR FAVORITE CUSTOMER. OR YOUR NEIGHBOR. THAT'S HOW YOU BUILD TRUST THAT STICKS.

CHAPTER 6

Beyond Social Media: More Tools That Actually Work

I used to think marketing was mostly about having the right tools. If your website wasn't converting, you probably needed a new platform. If social media was dead quiet, you just hadn't found the right scheduler. If no one was responding to emails, maybe a new software tool.

I kept tweaking things that weren't broken, hoping the *next* thing would fix what was really just a strategy gap.

Eventually, I realized: **the tools weren't the problem. The thinking was.** I was trying to build something using tools I hadn't thought through, out of a sense of obligation or FOMO because I wasn't everywhere.

And when I finally admitted that (after wasting money and hours I will never get back), things started to click.

That's what this chapter is about. It's about *how* to pick tools that make sense for your strategy—once you have one. It's about avoiding the all-too-common trap of over-tooling and under-connecting. It's about clarity, not complexity. Simplicity over everything.

Because when your strategy is clear, your tools can be *basic A.F.* and still perform like superheroes.

Here's what I've noticed after working with thousands of small businesses: Most businesses already have what they need. They're just not using it in ways that fit their voice, their goals, or the way their customers behave.

For example—if your ideal clients are Gen Z or Millennials and you're still relying on long, wordy emails or posts on Facebook, that's a mismatch.

If your business cards look like 1994 but your brand vibe is fun and modern, that's a mismatch.

This chapter's here to help you fix that.

We're not going to talk about *every* tool. We're going to talk about the ones that actually matter. The ones that give your customer a way to connect, feel something, and take action.

And just one more thing before we dig in: your tools don't have to do all the things. You need tools that fit *you*—your energy, your audience, your goals.

We'll talk more about strategy (which ties all of this together), but for now, let's walk through the tools that can actually help you show up, connect better, and be unforgettable—without adding more noise to your life or theirs.

Your Website (aka Your Brand's HQ)

Applies All 6 Brandship™ Traits

I used to think my website had to be super corporate looking. I modeled it after other speakers I admired. Mine was slick, black and white, edgy, high-design. Did it reflect the real me?

Nope. I was selling a bill of goods that didn't match who I was in person, or on stage. There was a huge disconnect. I thought I had to look like "them" (other professional speakers) to get business like them.

I remember the very moment it dawned on me that I needed to act like "me" to get the exact right audiences for "me." Ones who would love my message and the goofy but smart way I deliver it. Ones who would follow me, refer me, and support me like friends. Many have, in fact, become friends along the way.

I figured something out: your website isn't there just to impress. It's there to *connect.*

It's your digital handshake. Your "hey, this is us" moment. And it's the only piece of internet real estate you *actually* control without algorithms or ads.

But I've seen it so many times: small business websites that either read like a boring brochure or try to seem like they're a huge, multi-billion-dollar company when their real strength is their smallness.

Here are the typical pitfalls:

- Too much info, too little clarity.
- Too polished, no real personality.
- Or worst of all: just... generic. A template filled in with the basics and some stock photos.

You don't need the fanciest site on the block. You just need one that makes the right person go: "Oh. Yep. This is exactly who I've been looking for."

Let's walk through what actually makes a site work—and not just in a functional way, but in a *people-want-to-know-you* way. Every Brandship™ trait has a place here.

Relatable Websites: Say What You'd Say in Real Life

Your homepage used to be a digital brochure, but not anymore. That's the outdated strategy that most corporations still follow. Your homepage should be a virtual version of you, opening the door and saying, "Come in! This is us, and you're in the right place."

Don't make people dig through jargon or read like they're decoding a legal brief. Talk like a person. Write like a person.

- **Instead of this:**
  "We're a full-service dental office providing patient-first experiences." ("Full-service" is a huge pet peeve of mine!)

  Say:
  "Haven't been to the dentist in a while? No lectures, no guilt trips. Just clean teeth and good vibes."

I mean, who *hasn't* put off a cleaning longer than they should?

THE SIDEKICK SAYS:

ADD A SHORT WELCOME VIDEO TO YOUR HOMEPAGE. DOESN'T HAVE TO BE PERFECT. IN FACT, IT SHOULD BE THE OPPOSITE—JUST YOU, OR A TEAM MEMBER, TALKING TO THE CAMERA LIKE YOU'RE FACETIMING A FRIEND. A FRIENDLY, CASUAL WELCOME MESSAGE WITH MAYBE A DIFFERENTIATOR OR TWO THROWN IN. KEEP IT UNDER 90 SECONDS, BE YOURSELF, AND PLEASE DON'T READ FROM A SCRIPT.

Trustworthy Websites: Make It Ridiculously Easy to Reach You

If I land on your site and I can't figure out how to contact you within five seconds? I'm gone.

Most people don't click around for fun. If they're trying to get in touch, don't make them work for it.

- Put your phone number and email *in both* the header and footer. On every single page. Add buttons in the middle of pages that say "Get in Touch" or "Let's Talk" and connect them to an email or phone.

- Add a simple chatbot, and feel free to name it. Gen Z and Millennials *hate* calling people. (And this Gen Xer would rather do taxes than leave a voicemail.) Even a basic "Hi! Can I help?" message makes your site feel more alive.

    - **Instead of this:**
      "Contact us for more information."

      Say:
      "Got a weird question at 11:47 PM? Our little chatbot buddy's here—and won't judge."

Unforgettable Websites: Be a Little Weird. Please.

You know when you land on a site and you immediately forget everything it said two seconds after you leave? Yeah. That's most websites.

If your site looks generic—change it.

- Use real photos. Not overused stock images of…you guessed it…perfect people doing perfect things.

- Show your staff. Your space. Your actual happy customers. Behind-the-scenes stuff is gold.

- Even better? Video testimonials. Real people talking into their phones, saying how great you are. More trust than ten polished blurbs.

- **Instead of this:**
  "We're committed to customer satisfaction."

  Say:
  "We'll do everything short of baking you cookies to make sure you're thrilled with our service. Actually... we might bake cookies. Ask us."

Differentiated Websites: Be So Specific They Can't Confuse You with Anyone Else

If your website could be swapped with your competitor's and no one would notice? We've got a problem.

People are scanning fast. Help them figure out *exactly* what makes you different, and who you're best for.

- **Instead of this:**
  "We offer services for families in a comfortable environment."

  Say:
  "We specialize in helping neurodivergent kids and adults feel comfortable at the dentist. Bonus: weighted blankets and noise-canceling headphones at every chair."

That kind of clarity and specificity that makes someone stop scrolling and say, "YES. This is it." Even if you don't have neurodivergent kids, I'm guessing you would like and trust this dentist!

Magnetic Websites: Make 'Em Want to Click Around

Okay, here's the goal: someone lands on your site and doesn't want to leave. They click around, they read stuff. They forward it to a friend.

That's a magnetic site. It pulls people in.

THE SIDEKICK SAYS:

TELL SHORT STORIES EVERYWHERE. LITTLE WINS. FUN FACTS. WHY YOU DO WHAT YOU DO. MAKE YOUR NAVIGATION MAKE SENSE. "START HERE" IS BETTER THAN "SUBMIT FORM." "LET'S TALK TEETH" IS BETTER THAN "CONTACT US."

- **Instead of this:**
  "Services"

  Say:
  "What We Actually Do"

Just... be a human. Be helpful. Sound like *you*.

Bonus Website Boost: Your "About" Page & FAQs Shouldn't be as Dry as Plain Toast

I used to treat the "About Us" page like an afterthought.

Turns out... people actually read this page, *a lot*. It's the second-most visited page on most small business websites. Why? Because people want to know who they're buying from. Seeking connection is deep in our DNA.

They don't care about certifications nearly as much as they care about:

- What makes you tick
- What your dog's name is
- Whether you'll be reliable to deal with when their furnace breaks at 2 AM

So ditch the stiff bios. Instead, make your team sound human. Include what they do *and* something weird, quirky, or unexpectedly charming.

- **Instead of this:**
  "Jessica is our Client Services Manager. She has a degree in Business and enjoys yoga." It's better than just her title, but we can do even better.

  Say:
  "Jessica handles client calls, paperwork chaos, and keeps the snacks stocked. She's also training to become a yoga

instructor, so yes—she *can* hear your posture through the phone."

Better, right?

Photos help, too—real ones. No stock headshots with the cloudy, fifth-grade school picture day background. Show someone holding a paintbrush, a plant, or a ridiculously oversized mug of coffee. Show them doing something they love that has nothing to do with work, like kayaking, rollerblading, or even napping (my personal favorite)!

Your FAQs Are a Secret Marketing Weapon

Most FAQ pages are basically a how-to manual. Dry. Repetitive. Forgettable.

But they don't have to be.

FAQs are your chance to show off your personality *and* preempt objections. When done well, they build trust before the customer even calls. And they keep your inbox from being flooded with "quick question!" emails.

Make them conversational. Make them funny. Make them sound like you wrote them *after* three cups of coffee and one "you won't believe what this customer just asked" moment.

- **Instead of this:**
  "Do you charge for estimates?"
  "No. Estimates are free."

Say:
"Nope! Estimates are free. Also: we never charge for dad jokes, eye-rolls, or awkward small talk."

- **Instead of this:**
  "How quickly can I schedule an appointment?"
  "Within 2–3 business days."

  Say:
  "Usually within a couple days. Unless the zombie apocalypse hits, in which case we might be a little behind."

Also: sprinkle in a few unexpected questions that make people *want* to keep reading.

- "Will you judge me for how messy my garage is?"
- "Do you take bribes in cookies?"
- "Is it weird if I bring my dog to my appointment?"

> **Pro tip:**
>
> The answer to that last one should *always* be "No, please do."

Show your weirdness!

My best friend, Bonni, is a meeting planner, which is a saturated field these days. Her website has a page called 'Carpets of the World' showcasing the good, the bad, and the downright disastrous hotel carpets she's seen over her nearly thirty years in business. Why have such a page? Because it shows her personality and also says "I've seen a lot through the years" better than "30 years of experience to serve you" or something boring and typical like that. Check out her site at www.stellarmeetings.com. And hire her to plan your 25-200-person meetings.

THE SIDEKICK SAYS:

IF YOUR ABOUT PAGE AND FAQS DON'T MAKE SOMEONE SMILE AT LEAST ONCE, GO BACK AND TRY AGAIN. PEOPLE ARE HIRING HUMANS. SHOW THEM THE KIND YOU ARE.

Your site doesn't need to be fancy or perfect.

It just needs to answer the questions people actually care about:

- Who are you?
- What do you offer?
- Why does it matter to *me*?
- And how do I get started?

That's it. That's the whole job. It just needs to be done in a way that humanizes you and your whole team, and sparks emotion of any kind.

Blogs

So many blogs out there are just stiff, vague, SEO-stuffed nonsense with titles like "10 Ways to Maximize Your Synergy."

So how do you make your blog posts actually stick?

Start by having a take. Say the thing you actually believe, not the safe, echo-y version of it. Readers don't share vanilla—they share bold, funny, helpful, or even slightly spicy takes. Have a point of view. Be that person who says, "Hey, everyone's doing it this way—but here's what actually works."

Tell stories, not just steps. People remember stories. Even short ones. Did you mess up your email list once and accidentally send a coupon for 100% off? Tell it. Your audience isn't just there to learn—they want to *relate*. That's how you build trust. And it makes you way more memorable than "step 1, step 2, step 3."

Make it skimmable. Break it up. Use headers. Use bold. Use lists. Use real pictures of real things. Give their eyeballs a chance.

And again, for the love of all that is holy—ditch the corporate speak. Write how you talk.

Email (Not Dead, Just Horribly Misused)

I used to write emails like I thought a "real professional" should. You know—those long-winded, polished things that start with:

"I trust this email finds you well." (I *hate* that line today!)

Until one day I realized... I don't even talk like that. Why was I emailing like that?

Once I gave myself permission to stop writing like a robot, my emails got better. More opens more replies, more "oh my gosh, I actually read this whole thing" notes.

Email started feeling like a conversation again. Not a campaign.

And that's the whole point. When done well, email is personal, warm, and wildly effective.

Sort of. Let me clarify.

But First—Let's Talk Generational Divide

If your audience is mostly Gen Z or younger Millennials, you can skip this part. They're not reading email. Period. (Unless they're forced to for school or work.)

They'll ghost an unread message for weeks and reply to your Instagram DM or text in three seconds. So we'll talk about text and chat-based marketing later—because *that's* where they live.

But if you're targeting older Millennials, Gen X, Boomers? Email still works—if you make it worth reading.

According to a recent report, 73% of B2B buyers prefer to be contacted over email—double that of any other method, i.e., phone or LinkedIn.[26]

So yes, email still has a place. But it has to sound like *you.*

Use Email Like You Use Your Voice

Stop writing emails like you're applying for a loan.

If you wouldn't say it out loud, don't type it. And definitely don't copy/paste it from ChatGPT without rewriting it to sound like a human.

You're not just delivering info. You're showing up. Showing personality. Showing you care.

Instead of this:

> "Hello. We wanted to follow up and ensure you received our latest updates regarding your account."
>
> **Say:**
> "Hey—just checking in. Not sure if my last note landed. No pressure—just didn't want it to get buried in the inbox abyss."

---

[26] SoPro "The State of Prospecting 2025 report" https://thecmo.com/demand-generation/email-marketing-statistics/

Video Email = Next Level.

Want to really stand out? Start using video email. Especially if you're working with high-ticket clients or custom projects.

I use a service called **Dubb** for my B2B marketing. It's easy and has useful backend tracking. It's also white-listed, meaning your email doesn't end up in SPAM because you sent a link or an attachment.

I can see when someone opens it, replays it, or never clicks at all (which is *so* helpful. No more guessing.).

And these aren't fancy production videos. They're me, on camera, just saying something like, "Hi! Just wanted to introduce myself and tell you about my new keynote."

It's warm, personal, human. And it works.

Whenever I'm being considered for a speaking engagement, more often than not, the decision is made by a committee or someone higher up than my contact person. I always ask if I can send a brief hello video. Almost everyone says yes. I then record the video and speak like I'm in the room with the committee.

If I see the video has been opened, that's great. If it's been opened several times, that's really great, because multiple people watched it! Those are the speaking engagements I'm most likely to win.

The strange thing? I speak to chapters across the U.S. of the National Speakers Association, and share this with my peers. To this day, 99% of them still don't do it. That's so unbelievable to me, because it works so well!

Video Text = Next-Next Level.

Also consider video texts. They're the same thing, but a link is texted rather than emailed. Whether emailed or texted, be more like the 1% who actually do this – you'll see a huge benefit, especially in business-to-business sales & marketing. But even if you're B2C, this works really well, especially for bigger ticket sales like home remodels, cars, etc.

Imagine your mechanic sending you a text showing exactly what's wrong with your car. That's a huge trust builder, and it's becoming more and more common every day.

Your Email Signature = Wasted Space or Secret Weapon?

I have strong feelings about email signature blocks. So many of them are like a digital business card. Name, title, phone number, boring font. Done.

That's a huge missed opportunity.

Your signature block is *prime real estate*. Use it.

Mine has a fun photo (as you can tell by now, I hate boring, typical professional headshots), a "Send me a pic of your dog!" CTA (people do), and sometimes, a little blurb called "Three Unforgettable Things About Me."

Guess what? People notice. They mention it. They remember it.

So here's your permission:
Add something quirky. Include a hobby photo. Write a weirdo sign-off. Show you're a human, not just a vendor.

"But Shawna, that seems so unprofessional!"

Exactly. That's the point!

Coming up next: how to make newsletters actually worth opening—yes, even if you're not "a writer."

THE SIDEKICK SAYS:

IF YOU'RE SCARED TO SEND IT BECAUSE IT SOUNDS "TOO CASUAL," YOU'RE PROBABLY ON THE RIGHT TRACK. MOST EMAILS ARE IGNORED BECAUSE THEY SOUND LIKE EVERYONE ELSE'S.

Newsletters (But Not the Snoozy Kind)

I used to send the world's most boring newsletter.

I mean, it looked professional. It had headers, a banner image, some links. It followed all the advice I'd been given: send regularly, stay professional, provide value, don't sell too overtly or frequently.

And it. Was. A. Snooze.

Nobody replied, nobody shared it, and I barely wanted to write it.

Then one day I gave myself permission to burn it all down.

Now? My newsletter is called **Shawna's Non-Snoozeletter**. And it's the most opened newsletter with the most feedback I've ever gotten—ever. Seriously. More engagement than blog posts. More than videos. Even more than the obligatory toes-and-ocean pics.

People write back to say thank you. Or to tell me my dad joke made them snort coffee. Or to send me pictures of their dog (yes, really—every edition ends with a reader dog pic).

And all I did was make it *fun*. For me and for them. Feel free to subscribe to see what I do: www.shawnasuckow.com (it's at the bottom of every page).

A Newsletter Is Not a Press Release

Somewhere along the line, newsletters started sounding like corporate memos. Cold, stiff, and horribly professional. "Check out our latest offerings!" "Here's what's new at the company!" "We're having a sale!"

Ugh.

You don't need a fancy design. You don't need eight sections. You don't need to pretend you're running a Fortune 500.

You just need something that shows up consistently and makes people feel like they're in on something good.

Mine has:

- One short video tip on marketing
- One blog (usually an observation on a marketing trend I'm seeing)
- A dad joke or a "Deep Thought" reminiscent of Stuart Smalley (IYKYK)
- A featured dog pic from a subscriber
- A few random pics from my phone, without explanation.

That's it. Every time. Same format. It's got rhythm, voice, and my signature vibe.

Yours Should Sound Like You, Too

Don't copy my format, or anyone else's. Ask yourself: what would you actually *want* to get in your inbox?

It doesn't have to be long, or perfect. It just has to be *real and you-like.*

Talk about what you're seeing. What you're loving. What's weird or annoying or unexpectedly beautiful about your work lately. Be sure to include something totally NON-work related to humanize yourself further (like your latest Lego project or vacation pics).

My niece's best friend, Libby Schwers, sends out her newsletter, and I look forward to it every single time. I read and savor it from beginning to end. She owns a graphic design business, but she's also a crafter, a gardener, a candle maker, a home decorator, a bride-to-be, and someone who lives with a rare disease called Friedreich's Ataxia.

Libby shares her latest branding designs (which are amazing), a recipe she's tried, a story about her latest cool home or garden project, and other updates on her wedding, a trip, or life in general. Even if I didn't already know Libby personally, I'd feel as if she were a trusted friend. Subscribe to her newsletter to see for yourself how amazing her content, her work, and Libby herself are: https://withlovelibby.com/email-signup

How boring would it be if all she ever did was share graphic design tips and sales pitches to hire her?

Want another amazing example? I got you.

I connected with Alison Simmons on LinkedIn in early 2025 because I loved her humanized, fun posts about AI, caffeine, and family life in an RV. Alison is an AI business strategist and systems builder who helps entrepreneurs automate their mind-numbingly boring behind-the-scenes processes so they can focus their time on the good stuff.

Alison has a newsletter called The Caffeinated Entrepreneur, and it's fantastic. It's the only other one besides Libby's that I read religiously. It's got real business value, relatable life stories, belly laughs, and heart. Read just one of them, and you feel like you know her. *That's what we're going for!* Check out Alison's newsletter at https://thecaffeinatedentrepreneur.com.

Call It Something Fun

Naming your newsletter something a little different can work magic.

"Shawna's Non-Snoozeletter" makes people curious right away. It gives them a reason to open. It promises something other than blah blah blah.

You could call yours:

- The Monday Morning Rant
- Beyond the Boardroom (executive coach)

- Tales From the Dark Room (photographer)
- Tellers' Tales & Tidbits (bank)

Anything but "February Newsletter." Pro Tip: Use ChatGPT to brainstorm for this!

Newsletters don't need to sell; they need to connect. They're the regular outreach that reminds people you're still here, still interesting, still *you*. It doesn't mean you can't share your excitement about an upcoming product release or sale, but keep those low-key and not front and center.

When the timing's right, you'll be the one they remember, buy from, and refer.

THE SIDEKICK SAYS:

IF YOU'RE DREADING WRITING IT, YOUR READERS WILL DREAD READING IT. MAKE IT FUN TO CREATE—AND IT'LL BE MORE FUN TO READ.

Email Drip Campaigns (Not Just "Set It and Forget It")

Okay. Let's talk about email drips. Or nurture sequences. Or "automated flows," if you want to sound fancy.

I used to dread writing them. Something about putting emails on autopilot felt cold to me. The ones I receive seem bothersome and formulaic—two things I never want to be to my prospects right out of the gate.

If you've ever set one up and immediately wanted to delete the whole thing after reading it out loud? Same.

But eventually, I realized drip campaigns don't have to be pushy, annoying, or fake. They can be thoughtful. Helpful. *Strategic*, yes—but also *kind, humanized, brief, and fun.*

The trick is to stop thinking of them as sales sequences, and start thinking of them as **relationship builders**.

What Even Is a Drip Campaign?

It's a series of pre-written emails that get sent out over time, (hopefully) sent automatically, triggered by a specific action. Like:

- Signing up for your freebie
- Booking a consultation
- Downloading your pricing guide

That triggers a drip campaign that brings them along at intervals of your choosing.

They also can be used for cold outreach to new prospects.

So no, this isn't your regular newsletter. This is the stuff that goes out behind the scenes while you're doing your actual job. You write it once, set it up, and then it keeps working for you.

That's the magic—when it's done right.

The Real Goal? Make People Feel Seen

Each drip should feel like a natural extension of whatever came before it. Not a "HEY BUY NOW" ambush.

You're trying to move someone from curious to comfortable. From "who is this?" to "hey, I like this company."

That might mean your first email is just a friendly welcome. The next one answers a common question. The next tells a short story. The next offers a helpful resource of some kind. The last one invites a reply, connection, or soft ask of some kind.

And No, They Don't Have to Be Long

Actually, shorter is better. I learned this through A/B testing of my own, and it actually was quite disappointing at the time.

I really was hoping to prove the point that hilarity beats directness and brevity. I created two different campaigns and split my list of about 1,000 unresponsive contacts in half.

The first 500 received a sequence of five funny, longer emails with equally funny subject lines. One subject line was, 'My Mom Said to Reach Out'. The body of the email spoke of how, if they hired me to speak at their conference, I would win the distinguished Favorite Child award at Thanksgiving. All five were similar in tone (but with different tales, not about my mom).

The second list of 500 received a more direct approach. The subject line was simply the name of their conference.

To my disappointment, the short, direct approach won with my audience. Why? Because my audience is busy meeting planners who are bombarded daily with emails requiring attention and action, and many of the emails are fires they have to put out. The subject line with their conference name in it was something they *had* to open and read, in case it was just such a fire.

The body of the email asked two short questions that were easy for them to answer quickly, which many did.

The drip campaign went like this:

Email #1: The body of the email had a short, simple ask: are they the correct contact person, and when was the best time to send them my information to be considered as a speaker?

NOTE: If they responded to any email in the drip campaign, they were removed from the automation and added to my CRM with follow-up details (there are lots of tools that do this automatically so you don't have to monitor anything). If they didn't respond, they got the next email about 10 days later. I varied the timing to be 6-10 days so they didn't always receive them on the same day. You never know if that particular day of the week is bad for them.

Email #2: Same two questions, asked a little differently.

Email #3: Something like, "Hey, I hope I'm not hitting the wrong inbox. If you're not the correct contact, could you kindly direct me?

Email #4: Acknowledge how busy they are, and that I'll try again in a couple months. Sometimes this last one gets a response out of guilt, or out of a desire to not have to hear from you with the same questions in two months!

Now, my audience is different from yours, so my drip campaign strategy of short/direct messages may not be effective with your audience. If you're reaching out to businesses, short and direct may work best, depending on the demographic and industry. If you're reaching out to consumers, it might not. You won't know this for your own unique business until you do your own A/B testing.

It doesn't have to be sent to 1,000 people to get valid feedback. You can send it to a sampling of 50 and you'll get your answer.

Keep in mind that your audience evolves and changes rapidly, so what's true today may not be in six months. If your email sequence starts to see fewer results, that's your indication that you need to change things up.

Some Tips to Get you Started

Most people are skimming emails on their phones, while waiting in line at Target or pretending to listen on a Zoom call. You've got maybe 5 seconds to hold their attention, so make every word earn its place.

If your prospect or customer triggered your sequence (as opposed to you doing cold outreach), you can have more fun with your sequence.

- **Instead of this:**
  "We're excited to have you as a new subscriber. Over the next month, we'll be sharing our proprietary approach to helping you achieve optimal wellness."

  Say:
  "Welcome! You made it. Next few emails? Bite-sized tips to help you [solve problem they care about] without needing a PhD or a full-time assistant."

Map It Out Like a Road Trip

Here's a little trick: before you write anything, sketch out where you want them to go. Like this 5-email drip campaign sent to someone who subscribes to your tips:

1. Fun/unique welcome
2. Debunk a myth or solve a problem
3. Share a success story

4. Offer a free resource with real value
5. Invite a reply, a call, or a next step

You don't *have* to do all that. Sometimes 3 emails is plenty. Plan it first, then write like you talk. You're just leaving a trail of little breadcrumbs for someone to follow.

The best drip emails don't feel like they came from a software. They feel like they came from *you.* And that's the point.

Example: A Real-Person Welcome Sequence

- **Instead of this:**
  "Welcome to the XYZ Consulting 6-week insights series."

  Try this:
  "Hey, I'm Shawna. I've been doing this long enough to know that boring emails can be soul-crushing. That's why this series is anything but! Here's what you'll actually get instead..."

Then follow with:

- A quick video introducing yourself
- A case study and a fun photo
- A short value tip that leaves them better than you found them

THE SIDEKICK SAYS:

USE PLAIN TEXT FORMATTING (WITH YOUR REAL NAME AND EMAIL) INSTEAD OF A DESIGN TEMPLATE. IT FEELS MORE PERSONAL AND GETS HIGHER OPEN RATES.

A Note on Tone

Remember: this isn't a sales funnel. It's a *trust sequence.*

You're building a mini-Brandship. That means:

- Sound like yourself
- Be consistent
- Don't oversell
- Give more than you ask for

This is where people decide if you're the real deal or just another nameless, faceless company.

Print Tools (Part 1 – Fliers & Postcards That Don't Suck)

Print's not dead. But it is often deeply boring and flawed in its approach.

Fliers and postcards are still wildly underused in small biz marketing—not because they don't work, but because most of us learned to make them boring. You know the type: stock photos of people pretending to laugh at a faucet, generic "call now" headlines, and clip art that makes your eyeballs sad.

So let's fix it.

Rule One: Use Real Humans, Please

People don't trust stock photos. We can all spot "generic friendly plumber guy" from a mile away. He's fake. He knows he's fake. We know he's fake.

If you're a plumber, show *you* on the job. Covered in dust or water, holding a wrench and a coffee. Grinning in a crawl space (plumber's butt discouraged - although you could make this hilarious with a blurred box over your heinie and a joke!).

Manufacturing company? Show people doing the work, or posed outside the building wearing their favorite sports jerseys (bonus points if there's one outlier wearing the wrong team's jersey, and everyone is sneering at him in the picture).

Rule Two: Kill the Corporate Speak

You're not "your neighborhood expert." And you're definitely not the only business who claims "top-notch service at affordable prices."

- **Instead of this (Plumber):**
  "Fast, Reliable, Affordable HVAC Services"

- **Say:**
  "We've rescued more overheated families than we can count."

- **Instead of this (Electrician):**
  "Licensed, Bonded, and Professional"

  Say:
  "Our wiring is prettier than your ex's apology texts."

Seriously—humor + honesty = a flier people actually read. Unprofessional compared to your closest competitors? That's exactly why you'll stand out. You'll be the they actually notice and remember. The others are all blending into what I call 'The Blandscape' and sounding exactly the same.

NOTE: when they fail to differentiate, that also ensures they have to compete on price alone.

Rule Three: Make It Easy to Reach You

Include *all* the contact options:

- Phone number (mention if it's OK to text!)
- Email address
- Website
- QR code

- This line: "We've got a chatbot too, if phone calls make you break out in hives."

Millennials and Gen Z loathe calling strangers. Let them reach you how *they* want.

Rule Four: Don't Waste the Call to Action

"Call now!" is tired. "Free estimate!" is redundant (because who's charging for estimates these days?).

If you can't come up with something great, leave the space blank. White space is a design choice that's way better than noise. There's no prize for Most Text on a Postcard.

Bonus: Want Them to Keep It?

Your flier won't get fridge real estate because it's glossy. It will if it's:

- **Useful** – "Checklist for what to check before you call us."
- **Funny** – "If your toilet hisses at night, it might be haunted. Or just leaky. We fix both."
- **Visual** – Photos of you your team's dogs wearing tool belts.

THE SIDEKICK SAYS:

A FLIER IS JUST A BUSINESS CARD WITH MORE REAL ESTATE. MAKE IT WORTH KEEPING BY MAKING IT WORTH READING.

Business Cards — The Conversation-Starter You're Probably Wasting

Yes, I'm talking about paper business cards, because believe it or not, they're kind of cool again.

Everyone's gone digital—QR codes, apps, tap-this-thing-on-your-phone—and that's *exactly* why a smart printed card stands out now more than ever.

Don't Do This:

- Name
- Title
- Phone
- Email
- Tiny logo

That's a forgettable contact rectangle. Not a conversation starter.

Do This Instead:

Make it human.

Add a photo of you *not* in a stiff blazer. Show yourself baking bread, walking your dog, drinking too much coffee—whatever makes someone pause and go, "Wait, I like this person already."

Then, remix your job title:

- "Marketing Consultant & Cake Tester"
- "Financial Advisor / Altitude Addict"
- "Copywriter + Champion of Over-caffeination"

Memory hooks. That's the game-changer.

And make it just as easy to contact you as your flier:

- Phone (mention if it's ok to text)
- Email
- Website
- QR code
- "Not a phone person? Try my chatbot."

Real Talk: What a Card Is Actually For

It's not just to "give your info." It's to make someone curious about *you*.

My philosophy about business cards is that they should be conversation starters. Imagine handing over a card with you skydiving on it. Title: "Logistics Analyst & Weekend Rock Climber." They're *absolutely* asking about it. And boom—now they remember you.

That's the whole point. It's not just a card. It's a tiny, portable memory-maker.

I have 16 different business card designs. A little overkill? Perhaps, but I use www.moo.com and you can have as many backside designs as you want. The front of all my cards is the same, but the back has a different photo with a unique question that sparks a real conversation.

When I exchange cards with someone, I fan the cards out and say, "Pick one." Typically, what happens is their eyebrows raise up and they get a little excited like it's a card trick. Whichever one they pick, I say, "OK, now you have to answer the question." *And they do*. Then they ask me the same question, and a beautifully memorable, human connection is born.

One of my cards has a picture of my daughter, and the question is, "Tell me about someone you're proud of." I get to see their eyes light up as they get a little emotional and share a story. Then, I get to brag on my daughter.

Isn't that better than a boring, old card that gets immediately tucked into a purse or pocket, only to be forgotten the next day?

THE SIDEKICK SAYS:

A BUSINESS CARD SHOULD START A CONVERSATION, NOT END ONE. IF YOUR CARD DOESN'T MAKE SOMEONE CURIOUS ENOUGH TO ASK A QUESTION, IT'S NOT WORKING HARD ENOUGH.

Text Marketing (aka The Only Inbox People Actually Check Immediately)

Email is great, but if you really want someone's attention quickly? You text them.

Think about yourself for a second. Those 651 unread emails? You probably let them hang out there for a week—or forever. But a text? You read that. Usually within minutes, if not seconds.

Stats back it up: **text messages boast up to a 98% open rate**, and almost all of them are read *within three minutes*[27]. That's not just attention—it's fast, personal connection (if done well).

---

[27] Sender (2025) www.sender.net/blog/sms-open-rates/

When Text Works Best:

- Appointment reminders (turns out, people forget stuff)
- Flash sales or same-day offers (when urgency legitimately matters)
- One-off personal messages to high-ticket prospects

Keep It Human (Not Robo)

Even if you use a fancy platform to send mass texts, you need to sound like a real person. I think we all know by now that you always need to get permission first, or it is a huge violation of trust, and depending where the recipient lives, it also can be a violation of the law.

Here's how to keep it human:

- **Instead of this:**
  Reminder: you have a mammogram appointment tomorrow at 10am.

  Say:
  Your appointment is tomorrow at 10! We know it's not everyone's favorite thing, but we promise to be gentle and we'll even give you a lollipop at the end!

Short, friendly, and actionable.

THE SIDEKICK SAYS:

KEEP IT UNDER 160 CHARACTERS. USE THEIR FIRST NAME IF YOU CAN. DON'T BLAST MORE THAN 2-3 TIMES A MONTH. DON'T TEXT AT 3 AM (UNLESS IT'S AN APOCALYPSE, IN WHICH CASE, CARRY ON).

Test every message on someone who will tell you the truth. If they think it's blah? Don't send it.

Surveys, Reviews & Testimonials

I used to think surveys and testimonials were just basic and boring. Like a generic "how was your visit?" questionnaire.

Turns out, if your ask is unique and the questions are humanized, people feel more compelled to complete it, and you'll get real feedback that matters.

If you have a physical space, at checkout, place a printed card with a QR code that says:

"Got a sec? For every review we receive, a dollar goes into our Toys for Tots fund." Add a pic of last year's toy drive to increase effectiveness.

Instead of "some faceless box asking me to fill out a form," people think, "Oh, how cool. I can do that."

Do the same in email:

"Fill out this quick form and Henry our shop pup gets an extra belly rub."

Trust me, it's hugely effective. They're kinder, and they'll even add little stories about how you helped turn their week around or solve their issue.

Ask Smarter Questions

- **Instead of this:**
  "How would you rate your experience (1–5)?"

  Try this:
  "What problem brought you in today, and how did we help solve it?" That one tiny shift gives you gold for marketing, and more importantly, shows you care.

Online Reviews – Ask the Right People

Nothing moves the needle like a 5-star review. When someone thanks you in person? That's your cue.

"Hey, I'm so glad it worked out! Would you mind dropping a quick review? Here's the link—it'll take 30 seconds, and it helps more than you know."

Make it easier by telling them what helps most:

"If you could mention how fast we were or how friendly the tech was, that'd be awesome." Specific reviews help *you* and help Google and Yelp users *trust* you.

Testimonials – Record the Moment

Video testimonials are powerful—but waiting until later sucks the life out of them.

When someone tells you how happy they are, whip out your phone and say:

"Would you mind repeating what you just said into my phone for a quick video?" When I ask this, I almost always get a yes.

Ask permission to share it. Then post the clip on your site, on social, in your emails.

Keep Your Social Proof Fresh

Static testimonials gather dust. They don't help Google, and they don't help people who see them a year later.

So create a page on your website called "Cool Customers" or "Social Proof." Drop in fresh quotes and videos as soon as you get them.

Google *loves* active pages with real content updates. And potential clients love seeing life and faces—not just stale text.

THE SIDEKICK SAYS:

IF YOU ASK SOMEONE TO SHARE A MOMENT WHEN THEY ACTUALLY FELT IT, YOU'LL GET SOMETHING REAL BACK, AND REAL IS WORTH SHARING.

Swag That Doesn't Suck

Let's talk about branded merch.

Not the "I spent $800 on branded pens and no one remembers" kind. The good kind. The *actually-useful, slightly-weird, definitely-fun, builds-my-brand* kind.

Swag gets a bad rap because 90% of it ends up in the trash, but done right? It's fantastic.

The Golden Rule: Make People Want to Keep It

Swag should do one or more things:

1. Be useful
2. Be funny
3. Start a conversation

If it does all three? You win.

Think beyond pens, magnets, and keychains. Those are fine (sometimes), but they're forgettable. What's unforgettable is something that feels *thoughtful, clever, or just plain useful.*

Great Swag Ideas That Get Noticed

Here are a few favorites I've seen (or personally received and kept forever):

- **A kitchen towel from a real estate agent** that said "Because this home doesn't clean itself."
- **Dog poop bag holders** from a dog trainer with the tagline "We've got your back end."
- **Mini notebooks** from a coach labeled "Million-dollar ideas only."
- **A little screwdriver set** from an HVAC tech that said "For the stuff you can fix without calling us."
- **A tiny teddy bear** strapped into a child's car seat by an auto-repair shop as a surprise to its customer (this one came from one of my brilliant audience members and his customers love it).

Things that make people *laugh*, or *use* them, or *share* them on social media. That's the trifecta.

Bonus: The Referral Magnet Effect

Want people to *share* your swag?

- Add a little card that says, "Loved this? We've got more—just ask."
- Put an inside joke or mini challenge on it: "If you got this, you're officially in the Cool Club. Tell us at your next visit and get another surprise."
- Give them a reason to hand it to a friend: "Refer a friend and our receptionist, Barb, gets to add another flamingo to her desk collection.

What About TV and Radio Ads?

Full disclosure—I'm not a media buyer or a commercial production expert. But I *do* know what makes a message stick, and that's the part that matters here.

Because even if you're using "traditional" media, the same rules apply:

- **Be conversational.** If your radio ad sounds like it was voiced by a game show host from the 1970s... start over.
- **Skip the polish.** Listeners and viewers are allergic to perfection right now. Imperfect is actually more believable. Go for *human* over *Hollywood*.
- Speak like your audience talks. No corporate-ese, no jargon.

- **Skip the salesyness.** If it's overly scripted or too 1990s-used-car-salesman feeling (no offense to used car salespeople of today). The same applies here as before: no fake urgency or scarcity, no cliche call-to-action ("Call now for your free in-home estimate!").
- **Don't repeat yourself into oblivion.** That old-school "say the phone number three times" rule? Honestly, most of us aren't dialing numbers we heard once in the car anymore (same goes for phone numbers on billboards). Because Google exists and we're going to research you before reaching out, anyway, so don't bother with the contact details...seriously!

Speaking of repetition, I have to tell the story of the HVAC brothers who shall remain anonymous. I was binge-watching a series on a platform that was ad-based (ugh).

The first commercial was of these two brothers in a fun ad where they're playfully and competitively running the bases at the local stadium. It wasn't overly scripted, and was memorable. Twenty minutes later, the next commercial break came. The same ad appeared. I'm not exaggerating when I say that I was forced to watch that same ad about a dozen times that evening.

Now, I've never met these brothers, but if I ever need HVAC services, I will remember them for the wrong reasons, and then call someone else! Sorry, brothers!

Location-Based Marketing: If You Only Get One Shot, Make It Weird (In a Good Way)

Let's talk about the weird, wonderful world of location-based marketing: billboards, sandwich boards, bathroom stall ads, and my personal favorite—chalkboard signs with attitude.

These are your "one shot" moments (or more if you have a squirrel-size bladder like me, and therefore see a lot of bathroom stall ads). You're not in someone's inbox where you can try again next Tuesday. You've got one chance to catch a stranger's eye, make them stop for half a second, and maybe even remember you.

That means this is *not* the time for:

- Overused words like "trusted," "locally owned," or "serving your ____ needs."
- Generic photos that look like they were stolen from a brochure in 2003.
- Jargon nobody understands. ("We specialize in full-spectrum integrated alignment solutions"... cool. What's that mean?)

If someone's walking by, driving by, or in a bathroom stall, you want your message to spark something. A laugh, a nod, a "wait, what?" moment that breaks their pattern just long enough to make you unforgettable.

Location-based golden rules:

- **Say one thing, clearly.** This is not the time for a paragraph.
- **Be emotionally unexpected.** Humor works. So does curiosity. Weird wins here.
- **Use your voice.** If it wouldn't sound like you in real life, don't put it on a wall.

And don't forget visuals: if you're using a billboard or poster, the image should earn its real estate. If it's just a stock photo of smiling strangers in business attire, save your money and go hand out branded pudding cups instead. (Honestly, that might work better.)

Some of my favorite IRL examples:

- A chalkboard sign outside a bookstore at the Minneapolis airport that read, "World's Closest Bookstore". I laugh every time I see it, because at that moment, it's true.
- The tongue-in-cheek billboards from local, Minnesota-based Sherman Pole Buildings that went viral nationwide: "Quality Erections Since 1976". I mean...it's eye-catching and unforgettable, right?
- The billboard with a REALTOR® holding an ice cream cone, that said (I'm paraphrasing because I haven't seen it since, but it clearly holds real estate in my brain two years later): "This will taste so much better in your new home." SO much more unforgettable than every other real estate agent who

has their boring, posed photo with their logo and name...and a phone number I'll never catch anyway while driving 65 mph.

Your Waiting Room/Lobby is Marketing (For Better or Worse)

If you're a medical provider, mechanic, lawyer, tattoo artist, or anyone with a customer waiting room, let's talk about the most underutilized marketing asset in your entire business: your customer lounge. You've got a captive audience, and yes, they're likely already customers, but it's a fantastic opportunity to build trust and referrals.

In a recent keynote to 4,000 auto repair shop owners, I reminded the audience that **everything your customers see, hear, and feel is marketing**—including your waiting area. Think of it like your brand's living room. It's either saying "Come on in, we see you, we care," or it's saying "We had five minutes in 2018 to throw this together."

You don't need to spend a fortune, but you do need to be intentional. Because when your customers are stuck in that room waiting for their car, or their dog, or their surgery—they're absorbing *everything*.

And trust me, coffee and a TV playing your ads on repeat are not what I'm talking about (I'm looking at you, dentists and med-spas everywhere!).

So instead, ask yourself:

- What would *you* want if you were waiting?
- What would surprise and delight someone in a way that feels human?
- What would actually make your business feel *different* from the six others down the street?

One repair shop owner I spoke with became known as "the cookie place" because his wife (and his mother before her) bakes 30 dozen cookies a week, and every customer gets one. That's a differentiator I fully support!

Another audience member shared that he has an autistic son who loves Legos, so he has Legos in a kids' play area in his waiting room. I hope he has a sign explaining that his waiting room is neurodivergent-kid-approved! That's the kind of thoughtful touch that parents will share with other parents.

These little touches? They build trust. They make you unforgettable. They give people a story to tell about your business that leads to referrals.

Your waiting room isn't just a place to pass time. It's a captive audience hungry (see what I did there?) for something unforgettable and unique. Don't let it go to waste.

Make the Boring Stuff Awesome: Phone Greetings, Auto-Replies, and e-Receipts That Don't Suck

Let's talk about the unglamorous stuff. The things that live in the "eh, just get it done" folder of your business brain.

Each one of these are tiny moments that most businesses ignore—and that's exactly why they're ripe for differentiating, building trust, and being unforgettable, because if you're the rare business to do it, you stand out.

Your Phone Greeting

If someone calls your business and hears a robotic voice droning, "Thank you for calling [Generic Company Name], your call is very important to us..." they've already tuned out. Or worse, assumed you're just like everyone else.

Instead, make it sound like a real person. A warm, welcoming, *unforgettable* one.

Example upgrade:
"Hi there! You've reached Bob's Auto. We're probably under a hood or covered in grease, but we'd love to help you out. Leave a message and we'll call you back as fast as we can—faster than your cousin's unreliable pickup, we promise."

See? Human, warm, and fun. Way more unforgettable than the typical greeting we all know and hate.

Your Auto-Replies

Whether it's a Facebook message, a chatbot, or an out-of-office email--this is another moment to stand out. Use humor, transparency, or helpfulness. Just one is enough to stand out.

Example upgrade:
"Hey there! We got your message. We're probably with a furry customer. We'll get back to you shortly—thanks for being patient!"

Or...
"Thanks for booking your appointment. We'll see you soon—bring your appetite, because we'll have fresh baked cookies!" See how I just can't seem to forget the cookies?

Your Order Confirmations, Invoices & Receipts

This is the most ignored piece of customer communication—and also one of the most opened. Seriously, almost 100% open rate. Your newsletter has FOMO.

So why are most receipts cold, awkward, and designed like a drug store printout?

Instead, use this space to build trust, say thanks, and leave a final impression that doesn't feel like a transaction.

Example upgrade:

Check out this brilliant order recap email sent to my friend, Ava, from a company called Routine Wellness:

Ava, you did it!

It was just a Routine day at our office when all of a sudden, Ruby jumped on top of her desk and looked at the entire office in disbelief. “We’ve officially made it,” she said – “Ava just ordered from us!”

The entire office erupted in applause, and Sam did a plank for three minutes to work off some of the adrenaline she was feeling. “Don’t Stop Believing” started blaring from the speakers as we popped a bottle of champagne and raised a glass to you.

Ava, we’re genuinely excited that you’re a customer. Thank you for your support. As soon as we’re done celebrating, we’ll send you tracking information so that you can track your package. If you have any questions about your order, please reach out to us at http://routinecos.com.

Why This Works

Because these otherwise mundane communications are actually huge opportunities to build connection. Every touchpoint is a chance to:

- Reassure your customer
- Reinforce your personality
- Leave a positive emotional footprint

Don’t treat them like chores. Treat them like conversations.

Even a receipt can be marketing. Even an auto-reply can be unforgettable. And every one of them can make someone feel like they're dealing with a real person—not a system.

The Power of the Note

You know that moment when you open something you ordered and there's a *handwritten* note inside? You pause, you smile. You might even read it twice. Because most packages arrive with a generic "Thanks for your purchase" or worse—*nothing at all*—a notecard feels like a hug in a box.

It doesn't need to be fancy. It doesn't need to be long. It just needs to sound like you, and remind your customer that a *real human* packed that order with care.

What Makes a Notecard Unforgettable?

- **Real handwriting, real ink.** Even if it's messy. Especially if it's messy.
- **Use their name.** You've got it—use it.
- **Say something beyond "thank you."** Thank-you is great. But a personal sentence is magic.

Example:
"Lisa—Thanks for supporting our little shop. You rock!"

Or:

"Brandon, just a heads up—we included a quick-start tip sheet with your gadget. Hope it saves you from yelling at it!"

Want to Go Next-Level?

- Include a **small bonus**—a sticker, a magnet, etc.
- Add a **repeat-customer nudge**: "P.S. Come back anytime. We'll be here with more good vibes—and maybe snacks."
- If it fits your brand, include humor: "This package was sealed with love and mild panic. Enjoy!"

Why This Works

Because surprise + effort = loyalty. Most customers expect the bare minimum. When you go above it—even just a little—they don't forget.

Plus, it gives them something to post. Unboxing moments go viral for a reason. A notecard might be the thing that turns your package into a story they share. I know, because I've done it multiple times.

Alex & Andy: A Company on a Mission

I ordered a t-shirt I saw on TikTok, half because I loved the shirt's saying, and half because I loved the story of the founders.

Here's how one of their customers described them on Facebook:

"Alex & Andy is one of my favorite small shops, not just for their adorable pet bandanas and tees, but for the heart behind it all. 🤍 Sophie Wyrick started the business in honor of her Uncle Andy, a kind and generous man who suffered a life-altering stroke in 2020. When Andy could no longer care for his beloved dog, Alex, Sophie stepped in. Now, every order supports Andy's recovery, he helps with design, writes thank-you notes, and finds purpose in the process." 🐾

From their website (http://alexandandypetbandanas.com) Sophie writes:

"What started as a fundraiser on TikTok for Andy that went viral, has now become a small business with a charitable purpose, to inspire other stroke survivors and to give Andy a purpose again. Andy was a routine guy prior to the stroke, and loved his job, so I knew keeping him engaged and focused would be extremely vital to recovery. Relearning to write left-handed, Andy's hand drawn images are used on our custom designed shirts. He also writes thank you cards for each order."

I can confirm it's true. I received a note from Andy thanking me for my order. If Andy can do it, then we can, too.

This Company is Nuts!

I recently ordered for the first time from Udderly Nuts - a small business that makes specialty peanut butter (yes, I'm that person). Inside the box? Not just a jar (ahem...or three) of deliciousness, but **two noteworthy cards**.

This first card thanked me for my order, and featured a photo of Talia with her name handwritten below, her number of years with the company, and her favorite flavor. BRAVO! Simple, quick to customize, and *utterly* trust-building.

On the back of the card there was a micro-story about the founders and their mission, along with a coupon code for when I reorder.

The two upgrades I would recommend if they were my client: add a QR code, and another photo – maybe of someone in the kitchen making a batch.

And the second notecard featured a photo of the founders' family and asked for my help spreading (pun intended) the word about their peanut butters to other businesses—with zero shame in asking the favor.

I was instantly hooked. And not just on the product. On *them*. The people, the story, the experience.

The cards have warmth, and extra *effort*.

All of this shows me:

- They care.
- I'm not just order #8342.
- This is a business run by humans who value other humans.

In a sea of automated "thank you for your order" emails, this stood out *big time.*

This is the part of your business that the Big Guys can't fake. Their thank-you notes are printed by the tens of thousands.

What About Speaking as a Form of Marketing?

Ah...I thought you'd never ask (and you didn't...that's why it's last!). Speaking gigs can be one of the most powerful forms of marketing for small businesses—especially in B2B. Whether you're on a conference panel, leading a workshop, or hosting a webinar, speaking puts you in instant expert territory. You're giving value, sharing your brain, and showing up as the go-to in your space.

But here's where a lot of people blow it: they turn the mic into a megaphone for their services. Nothing kills a room faster than a 45-minute sales pitch disguised as a "talk." Audiences can smell it, and they'll tune out faster than you can say, "Let me tell you about our premium package." You don't need to sell from the stage to get leads. You need to be helpful, interesting, and memorable. That's what creates demand. People will come up to you after (or Google you immediately) *if* you give them something real.

So use that time wisely. Tell a story they'll remember. Share the mistake you made that taught you something they can use today. Offer practical tips and real takeaways. Make them laugh. Make them write something down. That's the kind of talk that turns a room full of strangers into future clients, podcast invitations, or inbox DMs that start with, "Hey, I heard you speak at..." That's how small businesses grow big reputations—by being the one they trust, not the one trying to close.

⚡ Action Steps

1. **Choose one marketing message and rework it.** Add personality and make it memorable or useful, or both.
2. **Build a fresh email sequence or a new business card design.**
3. **Rethink your newsletter.** Add things that have nothing to do with your business.
4. **Find a podcast or live speaking opportunity.**

CHAPTER 7

Simple Sample Strategies

I know this much is true: you need *fewer* to-dos. Things that actually work.

This chapter is going to show you how to actually use the tools outlined in Chapter 6—without needing a marketing degree, a social media manager, or a second pot of coffee every afternoon.

We're going to look at a few totally made-up (but very real-feeling) businesses that are in the same boat as you: from solopreneurs who are juggling way too much, to small teams that don't yet have a marketing department—*they are* the marketing department, to teams that have one person focused part-time or full-time on marketing.

These fictional folks all had something in common: their old strategies felt forced, too canned, and too complicated. They were trying to do "all the things" because that's what they thought they had to do to be taken seriously. But when they finally simplified—fewer tools, less noise, clearer messaging—they started getting more traction with less effort.

They finally felt like their marketing made sense. Like they could breathe. Like they didn't have to fake being bigger, flashier, or more "optimized." They got clarity. Confidence. Momentum.

And you can, too.

Here's what we'll walk through:

- Each case study will start with the Before—what they were doing that wasn't working.
- Then, we'll move to the After—the simplified strategies I'd recommend instead.
- You'll get a breakdown of the 3–4 tools that would actually serve that business, plus a few actionable ideas they (or you) could start using right away.
- I'll show you how "less but better" can apply to any business—whether you're a handmade candle wizard, a mobile dog groomer, or running a team of badass consultants.

Alright. Grab your superhero cape. Let's go.

Case Study #1: The Overwhelmed Remodelers

Business Type:

A small, family-owned home remodeling company with several part-time contractors and six employees—two in the field, one office manager, and the founder (who's still swinging a hammer half the time).

BEFORE:

Marketing Mood: Scattered, generic, and exhausted.

Tools in use:

- Facebook (with mostly crickets for engagement)
- A dated website that still says "Welcome to our homepage!"
- Monthly mailers with stock photos of kitchens and bathrooms and "Spring Special" coupons

Pain Points:

- Social posts were mostly "after" photos with captions like "Another happy customer!"
- Their mailers looked like everyone else's—smiling fake workers in hard hats and promises of "Quality You Can Trust."
- Leads were slowing down, and referrals weren't cutting it anymore.
- The owner hated marketing. Thought it was "not his thing."

What Wasn't Working:

Their messaging was too polished, too vague, and too impersonal. In short, too much like all their competitors—and they had lots of new competitors in the field since they started their business long ago. Their social media looked like a catalog—zero personality, no behind-the-scenes, no humans. Their website was hard to update and didn't have a single photo of the actual team.

AFTER:

Simplified Tools + Strategy:

1. **Website Overhaul:** One page. Yes, one. Clear copy with real language ("We remodel houses like we're going to live in them") and photos of the actual team. No stock photos. A short explainer video of the founder talking about starting the business 20 years ago and what's important to him.

2. **Social Media Strategy Shift:**
    - Weekly "Renovation Reality" posts: quick videos showing messy job sites, tool mishaps, and what *actually* goes into remodeling.
    - "Client Cameos": Reposting short clips from happy homeowners walking through their new spaces.
    - "Demo Day Diaries": Someone goes around for 10 minutes with a tiny mic, asking the demo team, "what do

you think about when you're doing demo?" or "what's the best part of demo day?"

3. **Local Email Newsletter (once a month):**
    - Subject line: "Don't Hire a Remodeler Until You Read This."
    - Included in every issue: 3 Red Flags with different topics each month, like 3 Red Flags when hiring a contractor, or replacing cabinets, etc. (done with humor and honesty). A fun tiny mic video from the previous month. A photo with "Lawn Art of the Month" honoring the hideous, the fun, the seasonal.

4. **Referral Strategy Upgrade:**
    - They started handing out postcards with a handwritten note: "Thanks for trusting us. We'd love to help your friends too—only the good ones!"
    - Bonus: They posted thank-you videos to their social media, tagging happy clients (with permission), building that emotional connection and reach.

⚡ Action Steps

1. Review your last 5 social posts—are they real or too perfect?

2. Identify one way to show the messy side of your business (people love it).

3. If your website still uses stock images or says "Welcome to our site," block off a Saturday or hire someone. You know what to do.

Case Study #2: The Boring but Brilliant Bookkeepers

Business Type:

A small, women-owned bookkeeping and payroll service focused on creative female entrepreneurs and small businesses.

BEFORE:

Marketing Mood: Sleepy spreadsheet vibes.

Tools in use:

- A very basic Squarespace website with stock photos of calculators and coffee mugs
- Occasional LinkedIn posts about tax deadlines
- A once-a-year newsletter reminding clients about 1099s
- Zero lead generation except referrals

Pain Points:

- They were attracting "anyone with a business," instead of their Exact Right Clients: creative business women with no interest in doing their own spreadsheets or tax forms.

- The brand didn't reflect their personality at all—they were warm, funny, and way more human than their marketing let on.

What Wasn't Working:

They were hiding behind "safe" financial industry language, which made them blend in with every other tax service in town. The site didn't filter for their ideal clients, and there was no real content strategy. Even their LinkedIn felt like a tax form.

AFTER:
Simplified Tools + Strategy:

1. Website Redesign with Niche Clarity:

- Rewrote copy to speak directly to "female entrepreneurs and small business creatives who'd rather do literally anything than open QuickBooks."
- Used friendly photos of their real team in their real office—complete with plants, snacks, and spreadsheets that made sense.
- CTA: "Let's be honest—you didn't start your business to track receipts. We did."

2. Monthly "Messy Money" Newsletter:

- Stories about real client wins ("How one designer finally got paid on time... every time.")
- Quick tips, fun accounting memes, gentle nudges ("This is your sign to call us for your quarterly strategy session…or you could ignore us until summer…but don't!").

3. LinkedIn Redo

- Weekly posts like "Things we wish clients told us sooner" and "Red flags in your books—and how to fix them."
- Occasional "Ask a Bookkeeper" Q&As with offbeat questions like, "Is it rude to invoice someone on their birthday?"

⚡ Action Steps:

1. Rewrite your homepage headline to speak to your *real* audience.

2. Rethink your newsletter.

3. Post one relatable "what we wish people knew" list to LinkedIn.

Case Study #3: The Internet Company That Actually Gives a Damn

Business Type:

A locally owned, rural internet and mobile provider with 20 employees, serving small towns and farming communities where the cows sometimes outnumber the people, and everyone knows one another.

BEFORE:

Marketing Mood: Corporate...but boring.

Tools in use:

- A forgotten Facebook page
- Monthly customer emails with service updates (read: technical jargon and outage apologies)
- Website was mostly text, no photos, and the words "high-speed" showed up 42 times
- Print ads that sounded about as interesting as a shoe rack

Pain Points:

- Constantly compared to bigger providers—even though those providers were impersonal and didn't serve the area well (or at all)
- Perception problem: "local" felt like "less than"

- Customers didn't understand what made them better, so they often went with the big-name company

What Wasn't Working:
Their messaging felt like it was trying to *sound* like the national giants—and that backfired. No one was telling the story of what made them *actually better*: real service, real people who are their neighbors, and commitment to places the big guys ignore.

AFTER:

Simplified Tools + Strategy:

1. **Website Revamp – From Anonymous to Neighborly:**
    - Replaced stock imagery with real photos of their install techs, customer service team, real customers, and local landmarks.
    - Added bios and quotes: "I'm Sam. I've climbed 198 telephone poles this year. Yes, I counted."
    - Simplified plan descriptions—no asterisks, no legalese, no bait-and-switch.
    - Shout-outs on social media to real customers around town—at the local T-ball games, the coffee shop, and the gas station.
2. **Facebook That Felt Like a Town Hall:**
    - Weekly "Tech on the Street" posts introducing one team member at a time with mini Q&As.
    - Reels showing behind-the-scenes: how they diagnose issues, what weather really does to rural service.

- Occasional "Rural Real Talk" about issues unrelated to internet, but important to the community.

3. **Customer Comms, Rewritten for Humans:**
    - Monthly emails rebranded as "The Community Connection"—short, friendly, and written like a neighbor wrote them.
    - Instead of burying outage updates in technical gobbledygook, they shared what they were doing and *why it mattered*. ("Yup, that squirrel chewed through our line again. He's a repeat offender. What should we name him?")
    - Highlighted a "Tech Tip of the Month" in plain English.

4. **Community Connection as a Differentiator:**
    - Started spotlighting local small businesses on their social feeds.
    - Gave away internet for a year to one nominated local family each holiday season.
    - (This one's my favorite) Made yard signs that read: "Connected by Locals. Not Big Corporations."

Action Steps

1. Rewrite your next service update like you're texting a friend—not writing a legal brief.

2. Schedule one "meet the team" social post per week with a fun Q&A.

3. Create a "We're Local, and Why That's Better" video for your homepage.

Case Study #4: The Landscapers Who Found Their Voice

Business Type:

A family-run landscaping company in the Midwest with a team of 40, offering full-service lawn care in warmer months and switching to snow removal and holiday lighting installs in winter.

BEFORE:

Marketing Mood: Practical. Predictable. Yawn.

Tools in use:

- Facebook with sporadic stock photos of lawns and snow
- A flyer every spring with pricing tiers
- "Contact us for a free quote" on literally everything
- Website? Basically a digital version of the flyer

Pain Points:

- Zero engagement on social media
- Winter services were always under-booked until mid-season

- People still said, "Oh, I didn't know you did lights!" or "Do you plow driveways too?"
- Owner hated self-promotion and felt awkward being "salesy" in a small town

What Wasn't Working:
They weren't marketing like they were a team of helpful humans. Their messages were focused entirely on tasks (mowing, mulching, shoveling) instead of outcomes (less stress, more joy, curb appeal that sparks envy from neighbors). And they were ignoring what made them different: year-round service, local loyalty, and a willingness to go full Clark Griswold on your lighting.

AFTER:

Simplified Tools + Strategy:

1. **Facebook Strategy—Seasonal Series + Faces:**
   - Summer = "Curb Appeal Wins" with before/after shots and client reactions
   - Fall = "Leaf It to Us" campaign with time-lapse raking vids and fun GIFs of blowing leaves into neighbors' yards or kids jumping into leaf piles.
   - Winter = "Operation Griswold" holiday light installs with family reactions and goofy blooper reels (these can be evergreen to use every year!)

- Snow days = "Shovel Shoutouts" showing plowed driveways with captions like, "Bob's kids made it to school on time. Be like Bob." (also evergreen!)
- A community give-back where they clean up an overgrown yard for someone in need each week in the summer, and plow driveways at no charge for senior citizens in the winter.

2. **Website Refresh with Seasonal Switch:**
- Header changes quarterly: "From Grass to Snow to Holiday Ho Ho Ho—We've Got You."
- FAQ page includes direct, clear answers with humor. ("Yes, we install holiday lights. No, we won't judge your six inflatable Santas.")
- Real team bios and photos, including one where techs are tangled in holiday lights, or laying in a pile of leaves, or making snow angels.

3. **Local Print That Feels Personal:**
- Dropped the price list. Started mailing postcards with a note: "If your driveway's a skating rink or your lights are still in the attic, we got you." Name signed in ink by a real person.
- Included customer photos and stories from the previous season (with permission).

4. **Referral Program—Sleigh the Season** (there I go, cracking myself up again):
- "Refer a friend, and if we light up their house, we'll light up your day (with cookies)!"

- Posted thank-you videos every Friday delivering cookies to folks who referred someone that week.

Action Steps

1. Plan four seasonal content themes that reflect what you *really* help customers with (Holiday stress relief? Time savings? Epic yard envy?)
2. Update your website to shift messaging with the seasons—no more “set it and forget it.”
3. Make one real customer the star of your next mailer.

CHAPTER 8

The Final Word (But Just the Beginning)

If you've made it this far, I want to give you a high-five, a cookie, and a nap. You read a *marketing* business book. While running a business. That alone deserves a parade.

And not just because this was a long read (I tried to keep the fluff out, remember?). But because what you just did—investing in your own clarity, your own voice, your own peace of mind—that's rare. Most small business owners stay stuck in the swirl of "shoulds" and to-do lists so long, they forget they're allowed to make things easier. Why? Because sometimes it takes two steps back to take a giant leap forward (over a tall building in a single bound?). And time is so precious. I get it.

I hope you're feeling a little lighter right now, and have a lot more clarity, like maybe you actually *could* market your business without hating every second of it. That's my wish for you.

Here's what I hope you fully believe now: you don't need to be like the Big Brands anymore.

What you need is a marketing plan that makes sense for *your* business, *your* life, and *your* customers. Something you can sustain. Something that builds trust instead of lumping you in with all your competitors. Something that's built by real people, for real people.

This chapter is the "end" of the book. But it's just the beginning of you marketing in a way that fits, and actually works.

Remember What Small Businesses Have That Big Brands Don't

Let's say it out loud together: *big doesn't mean better.* It means bloated. It means meetings about meetings, and endless "circle back" emails and marketing that take three months to get approval.

Meanwhile, you can change your messaging in an afternoon. You can test an idea this week. You can respond to a customer like a human. That's not a weakness. That's your *edge.*

Reflections from the Field

Over the past several few years, I've met thousands of small business owners—from scrappy startups in tiny towns to family-run shops with decades of success behind them. And I'll tell you this: the ones who thrive rarely have the slickest branding or the biggest ad budgets.

They're the ones who finally stopped trying to sound like a marketing guru and started sounding like themselves.

One woman I worked with—let's call her Nicole—ran a solo web design company while raising her young son as a single mom. For years, she mimicked the language of the big guys. Sure, she got business here and there, mostly referrals from people she knew.

Then one day, she started giving herself permission to talk about what it was like to be her: a single mom running a business between toddler naps. That changed everything! Guess who it really resonated with? Other single moms, other entrepreneurs of all kinds.

Another business owner—a gruff, no-nonsense HVAC guy—told me, "I'm not good at marketing." And yet... he started posting videos of his dog—a sweet pittie that tolerates sunglasses—riding shotgun while he went on service calls. Now people in his area recognize him at gas stations and ask, "Hey, aren't you the dog guy?" And fellow dog lovers look forward to meeting his doggo when he comes to their homes.

These aren't anomalies. This is what happens when small businesses stop pretending and start connecting. When they show up like the people they actually are.

The Pep Talk

Alright, superhero.

You've survived outdated advice, marketing hullabaloo, and possibly a mild existential crisis about your social media presence. And you're still standing, still building your business.

Here's the part where I remind you of something important: **you're already equipped for this.**

You just need to *start being visible in a way that feels like you.*

You've got a story to tell, customers who are rooting for you, and a business that deserves better than canned posts and boring professional language. So let your weird out. Show your face. Say the thing out loud, even if it's not "strategic." Especially if it's not strategic.

Start with one piece of content. One conversation. One moment where you ditch the script and say what you *actually* think.

That's when marketing gets fun. That's when people lean in.

You're not just small—you're agile, scrappy, and above all, you're human.

And that's your superpower.

Your FINAL, Final Action Steps

1. **Pick one strategy from this book to try this week.**
   Not all of them. Just one. (The simpler, the better.)

2. **Choose progress over perfection.**
   You don't have to get it right every time. You just have to get it *out there.*

THE SIDEKICK SAYS:

YOU'VE GOT THIS. YOU ARE THE SUPERHERO YOUR CUSTOMERS NEED NOW.

Keep the Momentum Going

If this book lit a fire under you—or at least made you want to *finally* do something with your marketing—don't let the spark fade. Please make use of the free Superpower Vault to help you keep moving forward! www.bit.ly/superpowervault or here:

Inside the Vault, you'll find:

- Dozens of downloadable files containing templates, AI prompts, story ideas, and more.
- My best marketing tip videos

- The ShawnaBOT: a custom GPT constantly updated with all my latest expertise. Ask the ShawnaBOT anything and she'll answer as I would, as best she can. Hopefully with a similar level of quirkiness and snark.

Want more marketing insights beyond the book?

Reach out! hello@shawnasuckow.com

Speaking (my favorite!)
If you want your audience to lean in, laugh while learning, and take real action after the event, that's my lane (plus, I'll keep them awake and engaged, so your coffee budget doesn't break the bank!). I bring outside perspective that shifts behavior, delivered with the candor of a true friend (the one who tells you when you have taco lettuce in your teeth). #NoBoringKeynotes

Business Book Clubs
I can pop into your discussion virtually, lead a session or entire series, or do an in-person launch or Q&A.

Marketing Superheroes Mastermind Group
A no-fluff, high-trust space where I lead small business owners in solving real marketing challenges and growing faster. Check out the vault to see when there's an opening to join.

Consulting (In Person or Remote)
If your marketing feels stale, confusing, or like you're shouting into the void (and it's not even echoing back...rude!), I'll step in as your outside brain and we'll get to the root of it and figure out what really works for your company (and you!).

One-on-One Coaching

For business owners or fellow speakers who want more traction and simplicity, my coaching is part marketing therapist, part strategy accelerator. We'll dig into what's working, what's not...and maybe what's been on that back burner for too long. You'll know exactly how to attract your **Exact Right Customers™**, and finally love your marketing.

One-Time 360° Marketing Assessment

Sometimes you just need a clear-eyed, no-fluff look at your entire marketing landscape. In my 360° Marketing Assessment, I audit everything—your website, social media, emails, swag, surveys, branding...bring it all on—to pinpoint what's helping you and what's quietly repelling customers. You'll get a detailed report delivered via Zoom so you can ask questions and really understand. Plus, my AI transcriber Bot (her name is Fatima), will send you a full recording with a list of recommendations and action steps. I'll give you the blueprint, you then go build it on your own schedule.

Whether we work together again or not—just know this: you're not doing it wrong. You're just done doing it their way.

And now, you're ready to do it yours.

This page left intentionally blank.
If banks can do it, so can I.

About the Author (hey, that's me!)

Honoring the O.G. Director of Barketing

My dog, Henry Jones, Jr. Even though he regularly ingested tennis balls and destroyed pillows, he was the best darn Director of Barketing this side of the Rainbow Bridge. He was the inspiration when I took the leap of faith to stop being so professional, and to start including dogs in my marketing and my keynote slides. See you again someday, my goodest boy.